TRANSFORMED THINKING

Loving God With All Your Mind

Edward M. Curtis, Ph.D.
with John Brugaletta, Ph.D.

WIPF & STOCK · Eugene, Oregon

Wipf and Stock Publishers
199 W 8th Ave, Suite 3
Eugene, OR 97401

Transformed Thinking
Loving God with All Your Mind
By Curtis, Edward M. and Brugaletta, John
Copyright©2000 Knowledge Elements
ISBN 13: 978-1-60899-589-9
Publication date 3/24/2011

About the Authors

Dr. Edward M. Curtis is Professor of Biblical Studies at Talbot School of Theology, Biola University in La Mirada, California. Dr. Curtis received his Ph.D. in Hebrew and Biblical Studies from the University of Pennsylvania. He is also the author of *Song of Songs* in the Bible Study Commentary series as well as a number of journal articles.

Dr. John Brugaletta is Professor of English at California State University-Fullerton. He received his Ph.D. from the University of Missouri. He is the author of numerous books, articles and poems.

CONTENTS

PREFACE

This book is the result of a number of years of teaching, interacting with students, and observing various parts of the Christian community. I have been troubled by the lack of interest in thinking within the church, and by the damage this attitude has incurred on those young people who seek to use their minds diligently in the service of Christ. I am also distressed by the weakness that neglect of the intellect creates for the church as it tries to resist the world's influence. It is out of a commitment to the idea that God has given us a wonderful gift in designing our mental faculties and that he expects us to use those gifts to the full that this text is written. I am worried by the idea, sometimes found in the church, that seriously using the mind and developing the intellect will get us into trouble and that true spirituality involves a kind of uncritical, unthinking mysticism where God simply directs us at every turn. It is with the desire to encourage every Christian to think carefully that this book is written.

Many people have contributed significantly in this project. My students at Biola University and Talbot School of Theology have taught me a great deal over the years and have helped me refine many of the ideas presented here. The students in Biola's adult degree completion program (BOLD) have patiently listened to the ideas and have read several different drafts of the material. They have discussed the ideas with me in class, usually with insights that have allowed me to significantly improve the work. It has been the enthusiastic response of these BOLD students that encouraged me to persevere with the work even when a number of publishers indicated that there is not sufficient interest in the Christian community to make publication of the material a profitable venture. I am grateful to Ken Oosting and JKO Publishing for their commitment to this project, as well as their commitment to adult education and their encouragement of thinking in the Christian community.

This book is not written for scholars but is intended for people who are serious about both their thinking and their faith. While the book is written primarily for college students, including adult learners such as those in the Biola BOLD program, it seemed necessary to use certain terms that may not be readily familiar to every reader. A glossary has been included to define many of these terms in the way they are used in this book. Terms included in the glossary are indicated by a superscript G in their early uses in the book.

Some ideas contained in this book were originally published in *Christian Scholar's Review* 15 (1986) and in *Faculty Dialogue* 21 (1994). I am grateful to those journals for publishing the material and for giving me permission to use the material here.

Biola University has encouraged me and supported me in this project in many different ways. They gave me a sabbatical as well as grants to work on the project during two different interterms. In addition, they organized and secured funds to support a year-long faculty seminar that allowed me, along with seven other faculty members, to teach half time while interacting with one another and several outside speakers on postmodernism[G]. Biola's commitment to this and similar projects for our faculty has been beneficial to this author and has made this book much better than it would have been otherwise. Biola and Talbot have also significantly contributed to this work by allowing me to regularly team teach a class called Psychology and Christian Thought with a faculty member from Rosemead School of Psychology at Biola. When Bruce Narramore originally approached me about doing the class, the administration was supportive of the idea despite the additional expense of a team-taught class. My interaction, first with Bruce Narramore and now with John Ingram, in that class has benefited me immensely in terms of integrative and Christian thinking.

I am thankful for the beneficent providence of ending up in the same Sunday School class with Dr. John Brugaletta. A casual conversation in which he offered to look at this material and make suggestions as to how it might be improved gave rise to a joint venture that has been a genuine delight. John has helped in the writing and in improving the clarity of thought and the flow of the material. He has contributed many excellent ideas to the work as well. I hope the collaboration will continue in the future.

Finally I am grateful to my wife Joy and my two sons. They always encourage and support me in such efforts even though writing takes much time that could be otherwise spent. I appreciate their patience and encouragement more than I can express. They are truly wonderful gifts that God has given me.

Edward M. Curtis, Ph.D.
La Mirada, California

INTRODUCTION

This book is about thinking. More than that, it is about thinking in a Christian way, thinking Christianly, having a Christian perspective in the thinking process. And even more than that, it is about developing a worldview—a unified set of assumptions—that is biblically based, so that we can begin to think Christianly.

But first we must talk about thinking. As with many other activities, some people enjoy thinking, while others cannot hear the word without feeling a twinge of anxiety or distaste. Everyone knows at least one person whose life seems coldly calculating, or highly intellectual but lacking in emotions; we often feel such people are missing out on a part of what it means to be human. Such extreme emphasis on the rational and intellectual to the exclusion of affection, pity, admiration, surprise, fear and awe is one extreme and clearly not normal or healthy. But there is another extreme, and that is emphasizing the emotions or feelings over thinking. Defining this extreme is more difficult, so let's imagine the following scenario.

Imagine yourself packing a suitcase. It is September, and you live in a warm climate. You are accustomed to wearing lightweight cotton clothing, and your instinct is to pack more of the same for your trip.

But wait. Where will your journey take you? To Anchorage, Alaska? The September days there will hover around a chilly 55 degrees Fahrenheit, while the nighttime lows will dip into the 40s. Better pack some sweaters, maybe a coat. They feel oppressive to handle in the present warm temperatures, but after just a few hours on an airliner heading north into the fall air of Alaska, they will feel as welcome as a good friend.

Most of us have lived through at least a part of this scenario. Many, however, go through only the first part, packing only shorts and T-shirts. If they are not to be painfully exposed to the elements during their trip, they either spend a great deal of money unnecessarily buying warm clothes in Anchorage, or they ruin their companions' vacation by constantly borrowing their clothes. These are the people who have failed to think, and whose understanding of reality is limited to their own immediate experience.

Then there are those who do think. They too begin by feeling heavy clothes are unnecessary, but they don't stop there. They read the weather page in the newspaper and see that Anchorage is considerably cooler than their home town. They then include this information in their plans. They pack sweaters and a jacket. Their vacation turns out to be a pleasant one; at the very least, they have not been an unnecessary burden on their friends.

Human beings are constantly engaged in situations which demand that they understand reality, even when reality is not obvious—even, that is, when it takes some thought. It seems to be an innate characteristic of *homo sapiens*, this process of observing the world and society, and then relating those observations to other things they already know.

Virtually every moment of our lives, we human beings observe things, and then those observations are registered in the brain. Sometimes we do this formally (a student taking lecture notes, for example), but more often we do it casually, almost without being aware that we are doing it. We use eyesight, hearing and touch as avenues of observation. In addition to these *senses*, we use the feelings we have about the things and people around us, those sudden changes of our interior weather that tell us, "Don't go in there; that place feels evil." or "This is a good place to be; I feel comfortable here." At times we think consciously about the process of observation while it is occurring, but at other times the process goes on without our being consciously aware of it.

It is possible, of course, for us to survive while not observing and recording reality accurately—that is, while out of touch with the basic facts of existence—but probably we would then be heavily dependent on those around us for the necessities of life. The man, for example, who has ruined his brain with drugs will survive (for as long as he *does* survive) on the charity of anonymous donors and the occasional soup kitchen. The patient in the mental hospital who thinks she is Eleanor Roosevelt is able to live only because she is protected by the hospital from the reality she cannot correctly think about. Both are out of touch with at least some of the basic realities of sidewalks and traffic signals, personal identity and private property, the day of the week and the historical era of their lives. The thinking of these people is so far removed from reality that we call them insane.

Most people's thinking is not so far removed from reality. In fact, when we take our car to a mechanic for repairs, we trust implicitly that he knows the reality of our car accurately. If he is *insane* about that, his erroneous work could drive us to distraction, or to the hospital. The physician must have an accurate understanding of the realities of our body, about its structure (anatomy) and its working principles (physiology). If he is out of touch with that reality, we could die from his prescription or his scalpel. Most of us, at an early age, learn to live from day to day within the basic rules of physical reality: we don't step off cliffs; we don't try to uproot large trees with our hands; we don't leave the safety of our car to pet the lion at the safari park. Or if we do, life gives us a swat for not paying attention to reality. For not using our heads properly, we may literally lose our heads.

Careful observation of the world and creative thinking sometimes lead to new discoveries about how things work, discoveries that result in significant advances in civilization. It was because of someone's observation of plant growth that we progressed as a race from a precarious existence of hunting and gathering to agriculture, making possible the civilization we live in today. Someone noticed that seeds, when planted in the ground and watered, became plants. Indeed, they became the same type of plant they had grown from. This discovery was momentous, no matter how simple and taken-for-granted it may appear to us today, having been taught it as children. This discovery and mastery of the technology necessary for irrigation made the unreliable practice of gathering wild grain and fruits a poor and inefficient alternative. And yet this advance required thought; simple, everyday common sense alone would never tell us that the long stalk of wheat, roots and all, actually existed in potential within the tiny grain of wheat, and that the soil, sun and water would release it in an enthusiasm of growth. Similar observations about animal propagation made livestock farming possible as well.

One could go on listing the milestones of human observation, thought and discovery: the realization that bacteria cause many diseases, the discovery of penicillin, the invention of the internal combustion engine, the understanding of the principles of flight and of electricity, the behavior of light—the catalogue is almost endless.

Just as thinking is vital to human beings as a species, it is of similar importance to the human individual, and Christians are not exempted from the need to think.

The Importance Of Worldview

This being so, it is important for the individual Christian to know as much about reality as possible. Our understanding of reality determines how we process new information and experiences, playing a crucial role in the way we respond to events. A witch doctor, for example, will see the illness of a sick person very differently from the way a medically trained physician will diagnose it. The first sees the world as animated by a multitude of spirits and will interpret the patient's illness in terms of those spirits, while the second sees the world (at least in part) as the interaction of chemicals and forces and will base a diagnosis on that.[1]

As a second example, the Hindu religion teaches reincarnation and the attendant belief that one's happiness or unhappiness in this life is determined by what that individual did in a previous life (before he or she was reincarnated into this life). The Hindu thinks of suffering and misery as both just and a necessary vehicle for one's being reincarnated again into a better life in the future. Because neither reincarnation nor its attendant belief (called karma) is part of orthodox Christian belief, a Hindu and a Christian will usually understand and respond to pain and suffering very differently, the Christian being less inclined to accept all pain as just and necessary. This difference exists largely because of fundamental differences in worldview[G].[2]

To take yet another example, both a naturalistic scientist and a Christian may be awed by the intricacies of the natural world. However, while the Christian sees the intricacies as evidence for a design and purpose in nature that points to an all-powerful Creator, the naturalistic scientist takes the same data as evidence for a random, purposeless world.[3] The first perceives an all-seeing God in charge of the universe, while the second perceives blind chance ruling everything. Again, these diametrically opposing interpretations of the data are the result of fundamentally different worldviews.

It might help us to envision the act of understanding reality if we compare it with putting together a jig-saw puzzle. Our problem is that, unlike the purchase of a jig-saw puzzle, we are not presented with a sealed box containing all of the necessary pieces; rather, the pieces are scattered throughout the world. The tasks that we humans set for ourselves call for us to find all of the pieces relevant to our particular task, all of the pieces that belong to the small part of total reality that we are considering, and then fit them together correctly.

Of course the task is an impossible one to perform flawlessly. The world of matter and energy, kangaroos and quarks, galaxies and viruses, is much too complex for any single human mind to perceive completely and accurately. Even communities of specialists — astro-physicists for example, or biochemists — though they know more collectively than any one expert knows, still are regularly tripped up by newly discovered evidence which reveals the falsity of some theory they had held. (This challenge tests their integrity as scientists for whom doctrine must give way to the evidence and not the reverse). This reason is not nearly good enough to stop thinking. We do not give up cooking just because we are not the world's premier chef; nor do we refuse to have children just because we will certainly make at least some parental blunders. In the same way, we must accept the obvious fact that we were created intellectual beings, remembering all the while that our intellects are as open to error as the rest of us. Just as our individual intellectual limits must not discourage us from diligence in thinking, so those limits should also alert us to the reality that the most comprehensive understanding will likely come as we do our work in community with others, each of us seeing aspects of the truth that others perhaps miss.

As Christians we have no less responsibility to think than do others, and it is incumbent on us that we *think in a Christian manner* about the many issues confronting us as we live today. The Christian's ability to think Christianly about every topic, every question, every decision requires that he or she develop a generally correct knowledge of reality. This correct knowledge of reality must be developed in a world that promotes many ideas and values that contradict those held by the Christian community. That is to say, we live in a society that holds a great variety of worldviews, many of which contradict or ignore the worldview of Christianity.

As Arthur Holmes has pointed out, thinking Christianly in today's world does not come easily. The task means "ferreting out the influence of non-Christian assumptions and bringing distinctively Christian presuppositions to bear in their place."[4] The purpose of this book is to suggest certain basic principles that are essential for Christians who hope to attain a biblically informed and properly Christian worldview. Such principles are necessary for the believer seeking to make significant progress in understanding reality and thus in thinking Christianly.

We live in an extremely complex world where we are bombarded daily with differing opinions and interpretations; it is a pluralistic[G] world where relativism[G] and ambiguity are important components in almost everything we do; it is a world where Christians are called on constantly to make decisions about complex matters with far-reaching implications and consequences. Without a biblical orientation, the believer is adrift in such a world, shunted off course by every current of opinion, and blown erratically by the shifting winds of intellectual fashions. We need an awareness of the process by which our worldview is established and refined in order for us to filter out extraneous elements that do not belong in the value system of a Christian. We also need such an awareness in order to focus our attention on principles and methods that will establish biblical truth more solidly in our hearts.

An awareness of our beliefs and values (both secular and Christian) does not come easily. Many, if not all, of the most basic beliefs of a society are rarely stated openly. They are often adopted by people at some level below consciousness and therefore usually go unquestioned. What is needed, to enable us to begin to see them, is to think about them consciously. We need to get our bearings by seeing and hearing them described and by thinking about the processes by which these beliefs and values are adopted.

I love to travel and have learned that it helps me to get the most out of my trips if I spend time before I leave becoming familiar with the place I plan to visit. Before I went to Death Valley a number of years ago I read several books about the area and its history. A friend who had been to Death Valley a number of times before went with me on the trip. When I told him the things I wanted to see, he indicated that he was unaware that some of the places existed. I was able to relate things that happened at certain places and understand the relationship between the areas and past events because I had become familiar with the place before I went there, and my friend was amazed at how much he had missed on his previous trips to Death Valley. My reading did not make the trip unnecessary, and there were many things that were quite different from how I had imagined them; the experience brought the place to life in a way that nothing else could. At the same time I would have missed a great deal of the benefit of the trip if I had gone unprepared. It is always disappointing to return from a trip only to discover that I missed one of the most significant things that was there. I hope this book will serve as a sort of travel guide for thinking Christianly and that it will help the reader to know what to look for as he or she lives life.

It is well known that our perception is influenced (and sometimes determined) by our worldview[G]. Scientists, for example, are trained to look for certain things, often causing them to find only what they are looking for. They sometimes fail to notice other significant facts because of the theories to which they had committed themselves, theories which, in effect, told them what to look for. Many scientific breakthroughs come from looking at the same data from a new perspective, one that was not included in a theory. Abel[5] tells the story of a museum director who was trying to determine the authenticity of a horse thought to have come from ancient Greece. After months of research and careful study, one day the director walked by the statue and happened to notice a line running from the top of the mane to the tip of the nose—a line that clearly indicated that the statue was a fraud—a line that had been clearly visible in photographs of the statue found in numerous books. He and others had passed the statue hundreds of times and had examined the object with great care on many occasions, but no one had ever noticed what, in hindsight, proved to be the most significant feature of the statue.

Thinking about the process by which we acquire values and beliefs and giving conscious attention to the values to which we are committed can cause important pieces of the *reality puzzle* to register with us, allowing us to fit them more accurately into their proper place in the scheme of things.

This book, then, provides an introduction to the process of working with the reality puzzle. We begin by discussing the process of integration, that process by which we put together in a harmonious whole the various pieces of information that come to us throughout our lives. Then we take up the importance of the assumptions on which we base our acceptance or rejection of information. Next, we look at modern and postmodern assumptions, showing how each in its different way not only offers a challenge and a danger, but also offers potentially helpful tools for Christian thinking. Having recognized these two mixtures of perils and aids, we consider the two modes by which Christian thinking itself acquires knowledge: special revelation[G] (primarily Scripture) and general revelation[G] (experience). Finally, we offer some comments and a few helpful hints on developing a worldview that is biblically informed.

Our hope is that the ideas presented in this book will help us to make the most of the journey as we live life. We need to know what to look for along the way as we try to develop an accurate understanding of reality; we do not want to miss significant aspects of reality because we do not know what to look for. We do not want to miss important signposts because we were looking for other things when we passed them; we do not want to miss those parts of reality that can easily escape our notice because they blend in so well with the scenic background. In addition, we need to be alert to danger signs and to harmful elements in the environment that can divert us from the right path and derail us in our efforts to know truth and live life effectively as God's children.

Notes

[1]This point is illustrated by an opinion piece that appeared in the *Los Angeles Times* on June 13, 1993, and a letter to the editor that appeared in the *Times* on June 23, 1993. The opinion piece was written by Johnny P. Flynn who teaches Native American religion at Northern Arizona University. According to Mr. Flynn, a disease that had caused a number of serious illnesses and several deaths on a Navajo reservation was, in the opinion of the Navajo medicine people, "the result of the young people

forgetting the ancient Navajo teachings" and "failing to protect the boundaries marked by the four sacred mountains that border and encircle the reservation." These medicine people were holding cleansing ceremonies to wipe away the illness. Mr. Flynn seemed quite suspicious of the claims of medical doctors who believed that the illness was a viral infection caused by droppings from rodents. Dr. Jarvey Gilbert who wrote in response to the original article argued that the problem would not be solved by tribal rituals but by proper hygiene. He says "The medicine men can perform their rituals, but no one who believes that germs and viruses cause disease will believe their methods to be effective."

[2]According to James Sire (*Discipleship of the Mind* [Downers Grove, Illinois, 1990], pp. 29-30), "A world view is a set of presuppositions (assumptions which may be true, partially true or entirely false) which we hold (consciously or subconsciously, consistently or inconsistently) about the basic makeup of our world."

[3]Reuben Abel (*Man is the Measure* [New York: The Free Press, 1976], p. 137) points out that what Darwin saw for the first time was an open ended natural selection, without purpose of balance or plan, in which anything might happen. This perspective is shared by many who are committed to naturalism.

[4]Arthur Holmes, *Contours of a World View* (Grand Rapids, Michigan: William B. Eerdmans Publishing Company, 1983), p. viii.

[5]Abel, *Man is the Measure*, p. 40.

CHAPTER 1

Integration—The Key To Understanding Reality

The story has been told many times, but it is such a clear image of the problem we are about to investigate that it is worth telling again. Four blind friends, none of whom had ever seen an elephant (or even a picture of one), came upon an actual elephant. One of the blind friends put his arms around one leg of the animal and concluded that what he had hold of was a pillar, probably one supporting a large building. Another blind man took hold of the elephant's tail and announced that it was a rope. The third man leaned against the side of the animal's body and decided he'd met a wall. The fourth sightless man touched the trunk and took his private evidence as proof that he had encountered a large hose, probably one belonging to the fire department.

The four blind friends then compared notes. Each insisted that his individual conclusion about the reality they were examining was correct and complete. In contrast with the monumental patience of the elephant, who seems to have quietly accepted the indignities of this examination, the four friends quarreled fiercely over which of their fragments of knowledge was the correct one. They ended, of course, by no longer remaining friends. The point of the story is that, while all four of the men were, each in his severely limited way, *correct*, all of them were so far from realizing that what they had touched was an elephant that all were about as wrong as it is possible to be. A person who believes an elephant is a wall or a rope is as out of touch with reality as the person who thinks his shoes are stray dogs and calls the animal control officer to pick them up. What the four men had *not* done was to integrate their separate perceptions. Had they done so, they would have come much closer to understanding the curious anatomy of the beast we call an elephant.

While it behooves every Christian to have an accurate understanding of reality, many seem to make the mistake of the blind friends in the story, each assuming that his or her individual perspective on an issue is comprehensive and exhaustive. In order to perceive reality accurately, we must first identify all of the relevant data, including data genuinely perceived by others, and then integrate all of that data. Integration, in this case, means combining facts in such a way as to form a complete, harmonious and coordinated concept. Integration, in other words, pulls all the facts together into an entity. It is the opposite of segregation, which in this context means the isolation of facts and then limiting one's concept to only one or a few of those facts. Isolation was the sort of thing the blind men did.

If reality were neat and came in symmetrical packages, integration would be simpler than it is. Unfortunately, it is all too easy to demonstrate that reality is not neat and symmetrical. For example, the human heart is not where we would expect it to be in a body that appears to balance every pair of features (eyes, ears, arms, legs), but place every single feature on a center line (nose, mouth); the heart is off center—though, as Chesterton remarks, God seems to think it is in the right place. But it's not neat; any sensible human who tried to build a robot would continue the pattern and place it on a center line. Likewise, the orbits of planets, like the planets themselves, are not perfectly round; they are ellipses, and not all of them the same ellipse. Again, the distinction between organic and inorganic matter becomes blurred when a tree's roots absorb minerals which have dissolved in water, transforming those minerals into wood and leaves. Reality is, in a word, irregular. It is unhandy for grasping by the human mind, though by no means impossible. It is even, we might feel, messy, though if we reject thinking on that count, we are rejecting life for life itself, its methods of propagation, its high rate of mortality, its mixture of successes and failures, and so forth, seems similarly *messy* in its local inaccuracies but overall appropriate direction.

How then can we know reality? How can we take its measure if it adheres to no pattern or standard? We can, and the way we can is probably best illustrated by a simple example from plane geometry. If we wish to find the area of a regular shape like a rectangle, we gather two pieces of data, the rectangle's length and width, and we multiply one by the other. The problem of integration here (determining the surface between a set of lines) is so simple as to be almost invisible.

But if the shape is more complex—with wavy lines as boundaries, for example—there is no formula that will give its exact area. We can come fairly close to finding its area, however, if we superimpose on the shape a more regular shape that approximates its size and boundaries, and then take the area of that by means of a formula. This crude method can be made more accurate by imposing not one but many smaller rectangles on the original wavy figure, approximating its shape, then taking the area of each and adding them together. The smaller the individual figures are made (that is to say, the more detailed information we have), the more accurate will be our measure of the irregular figure's area. To envision this last, think of a hollow gourd; fine sand will fill its irregular interior more completely than marbles or golf balls will. The mathematical process of integration allows the figures inside the wavy lines to become infinitesimally small and then adds them up to give an exact indication of the figure's area. This illustrates the process of integration: it is the process of adding up the small components of reality (reality being the irregular figure) so as to determine its area as accurately as possible. In a similar way, our job is to put together the various components of reality (the physical world, society, the spiritual world, and whatever else constitutes reality) in such a way as to give us an accurate understanding of what reality is.

Since our task requires us to learn what reality is like, it is important, at the very beginning, to understand how we learn. Then, in the next chapter we want to consider how worldview works and the sources from which we get the data we use in thinking Christianly.

The Ways In Which We Learn

We acquire knowledge in four basic ways: through empiricism, reason, intuition, and faith. To begin with empirical[G] learning, we sometimes see this take the form of experiments in formal academic research where precise measurements are made under carefully controlled conditions. Much more frequently, however, it comes about as a result of the things we experience in the world, primarily through our senses (some would even include religious experiences in this category). Empirical learning is the primary method of the sciences and constitutes a legitimate way to know truth. Empiricism has the advantage that we can, theoretically at least, repeat our observations to check their validity. For example, everyone agrees on the temperature at which water boils at sea level because, theoretically, anyone can travel to sea level with a pot, clean water, and a thermometer, provide a heat source and repeat the experiment. This feature, repeatability, is at the heart of the scientific method.

Often initial errors in perception can be corrected through further experience and observation. But information gained in this way is always somewhat tentative because it is impossible for us to observe the totality of reality and the portion of it that we observe might not be representative of the bigger picture. Even if the men examining the elephant had been scientists and had done detailed experiments on their portion of the elephant, their conclusions would still have fallen short of the truth because they confined their empirical observations to a small part of the whole and did it apart from an awareness of the bigger picture. The man who thought the elephant was a rope might have discovered eventually that his *rope* was alive, but he might well have concluded it was a snake, still far from the truth of an elephant's tail because he did not consider the rest of the whole phenomenon.

People often make the same mistake as the blind men in the story did. They somehow suppose that their observations and experiences are the same as those of everyone else and thus provide a clear picture of exactly how things are. Often though these observations are biased and quite limited, and others whose experiences and cultures are different than ours will reach very different conclusions. People often hold extremely dogmatic opinions on the basis of their limited observation and have difficulty accepting the viability of variant views based on the observations of others. Research done in the social sciences, for example, must be carefully designed to accumulate data from a truly representative sample of experience, and much effort is expended in those disciplines to identify and control as many variables as possible in order to prevent inaccurate conclusions about cause and effect. Such care in making observations is often lacking at the popular level and this frequently gives rise to inaccurate and misleading generalizations that reflect a distorted picture of reality.

Sometimes our personal interest colors our perception so that we miss essential parts of the data. I was recently taking my son to a youth activity at church. We were running late and my son was in the final stages of getting dressed as we drove down the street. I heard a loud cry of dismay from the back seat and said, "What's wrong." My son replied that he couldn't find his comb. He was sure that he had put it in the car but now he could not find it. He said, "Why is it that when you really need something you can never find it?" I replied, "That's Murphy's Law." My son said, "Why does Murphy's Law work?" I had never given that question much thought, but after briefly reflecting on it, I suggested that at least part of the reason is that it is generally only when we need something and can't find it that its absence registers with us. I said, "How many times have you combed your hair today, and how many times were you unable to find the comb?" He couldn't remember exactly, but he knew he had combed his hair several times earlier in the day and each time had found the comb where it was supposed to be. Here was the secret of Murphy's Law. Often it is only those times when we are greatly inconvenienced by something that is missing or by something that takes longer than we anticipated or by something going wrong at a particularly crucial time (all personal interests) that the fact registers with us.

Often we see only what we expect to see or have been trained to see and we miss other important facts and relationships that are part of the reality. Several summers ago our family decided to drive from California to Texas and then to New Jersey to visit relatives. My son, who collects butterflies, was especially excited because he hoped to find butterflies that are not native to California for his collection. He asked me several times about the butterflies that he would find in Texas where I grew up and I was unable to remember anything except a Monarch. When we arrived at my mother's house near Dallas, we caught thirteen butterflies the first day we were there, and these were not just small, drab specimens. Some were swallowtails that were four or five inches across and beautifully colored; others were smaller leaf butterflies that blend in with the bark of trees when they have their wings folded, but that reveal brilliant reds and oranges when they spread their wings. I was amazed by the experience. I grew up in that place; I spent twenty-two years of my life there, but I missed seeing all the butterflies that were there. It was only when I began looking for butterflies that I saw what had been there all the time.

Christians often have a tendency to select only the data that supports their claims to truth while ignoring problematic data. Job accused his friends of only looking at the instances where the righteous prosper and ignoring numerous examples of righteous people suffering or of the wicked prospering (Job 12:3-12; 21:7-34).

It is important to recognize that the empirical approach to knowing provides only raw data that must then be interpreted. Even the most well-designed experiment that identifies and controls all the possible variables only provides data. When medical researchers try to find out why certain people are more vulnerable to heart disease, they survey people who have con-tracted the disease, collecting information on age, dietary habits, genetic background, energy expended in exercise per week, and so on. But this collects only data. The researcher must then inter-pret that data and determine its meaning and relationship to other observations about the disease, just as any observer among us must integrate data with other segments of reality.

It is here, at the point of interpretation, that considerable diversity is encountered. Interpreters approach the data from different perspectives, often determined by their presupposi-tions, their discipline, or the theoretical framework they have embraced within a particular discipline. The perspective of the interpreter is also affected by culture, educational background, primary way of thinking, etc. It is not terribly unusual for two interpreters, both of whom are experts in the same discipline, to present radically different interpretations of the same data. One politician, bolstered by the opinion of a leading economist, sug-gests that a certain group of economic indicators indicate clearly that the economy is moving forward toward new heights of prosperity, while another politician, supported by a different prominent economist, concludes that the data indicates that the economy is in for major problems unless present policies are changed quickly. Data is the raw materials of interpretation; the same load of lumber can be used to build any number of very different houses.

The legal system is designed to bring forward witnesses who have knowledge about specific aspects of a case. People who have viewed a crime or an accident are questioned in order to determine what data they can contribute from their individual observational perspective. The system seeks to limit the witnesses' contributions to the data that comes from their own observation. They are prevented from interpreting what they saw or offering their opinion as to what transpired apart from their actual observation.[1] It is the job of the attorneys and *expert witnesses* to then interpret the data given to determine what it means with respect to the law. If it were possible to provide witnesses whose varied perspectives covered every detail of an incident, it seems likely that the attorneys would still present radically different interpretations of what happened. It may be argued that the preceding illustration is unfair because many attorneys have vested interests (their clients and their own reputation) that sometimes override the desire to determine the truth. But diversity in interpretation (though usually not spanning such wide extremes) is found in every discipline (and vested interests are not always absent in the realm of either popular interpretation or *objective* scholarship). Such diversity in interpretation is generally less in the concrete and practical areas of a discipline (e.g., most doctors agree on the effects of certain drugs on people with mental and emotional problems) than in the more theoretical and abstract areas (e.g., there is considerable debate among these same doctors about some aspects of the mechanisms of action of these drugs, that is, what exactly makes them work the way they do). David Wolfe[2] also suggests that the broader the application of a theory (i.e., the more data it seeks to account for) the greater will be the diversity in interpretation. There will likely be less difference of opinion among scientists about a theory that enables one to predict lunar eclipses than there will be about a theory that accounts for the movement of all the celestial bodies.

We also learn and know things on the basis of reason, a term that refers to the more orderly forms of thinking. People are capable of thought, and logical thinking can lead us to truth in various areas. The various forms of logic, both deductive and inductive, were developed by the ancient Greek philosophers, who articulated formal principles that constitute the backbone of much of Western civilization. Logic is the basis of mathematics, which relieves us of having to empirically determine what 2+2 is each time we encounter the problem. In deductive logic certain correct premises, when put together in a valid way, lead to true conclusions. For example, one might reason that, to begin with, all members of the Baseball Hall of Fame were great baseball players; next, Mickey Mantle is a member of the Baseball Hall of Fame. We can then logically deduce that Mickey Mantle was a great baseball player. This last piece of knowledge is the fruit of our deductive reasoning, and we have arrived at it without having observed Mickey Mantle actually play baseball.

Likewise, on the basis of inductive reasoning we can argue that if in a large number of cases, people with a certain disease are found to be carrying a virus that is not normally found in healthy people, the virus is probably the cause of the disease. But induction can only lead to a probable conclusion because it will never be based on the totality of the possible data. (The virus might depend on other factors to trigger its harmful effects, or its presence might be completely coincidental and irrelevant to the disease.) Logic is useful because it allows us to reach conclusions about things that we cannot determine empirically, that is to say, by observation. Nevertheless in practice logic is seldom independent of experience. Practical logic and associative logic are widely practiced on a popular level and in other cultures, and these methods lead people to an understanding of truth as well. (It is in fact this kind of logic that we often find in Scripture).

Logic, in whatever form, is always an attempt to organize thought processes so that they approximate, as closely as possible, the non-mental processes of the world. When we say that, logically, if A is larger than B and B is larger than C, therefore A must be larger than C, we accept the logic of the statement because it strikes us as the way the physical world works. But sometimes our logic is based upon incorrect or uncertain premises, producing unreliable conclusions, and sometimes questionable perceptions about relationships[3] (e.g., cause and effect) lead us to invalid conclusions. Despite the problems sometimes encountered in applying logic, it remains a valid means of perceiving truth.

A third way to perceive truth is through intuition. People through some apparently mystical insight see a truth that is not based on logic or empirical thinking. Often great breakthroughs in science are the result of unexpected and perhaps unexplainable creative insight that comes to an individual.[4] L. J. Henderson, in writing of medical diagnosticians, says

> More often than not skillful diagnosticians reach a diagnosis before they are aware, or at any rate conscious, of the grounds that justify their decision. If asked to explain the reasons for their diagnosis, they often clearly show by their behavior that they are obliged to think them out, and that to do so is an awkward task. This is true of doctors, of lawyers, and of men of affairs.[5]

This method seems to be common in the arts as novelists (for example) intuit the best shape for a plot or character, and in interpersonal relationships as people *sense* certain things about other people. Often decisions about people such as whether to hire them, whether to promote them, whether to like them or whether to allow them into our circle of friends, etc. are made on the basis of intuition rather than on an *objective* basis. Often those who make decisions on the basis of intuition seem to expect others to accept their conclusions, feeling they should be exempt from criticism and evaluation. This clearly constitutes a weakness of the method.[6] While some intuitions are shown in hindsight to be correct, many never receive that validation, while many claims to truth reached through intuition contradict one another. Thus while the method cannot be discredited as a valid means of perception, the method often goes awry, producing problematic results.

It should also be noted that often, when confronted by a new idea or theory, people react immediately to the idea because it does or does not *feel right*. There is an intuitive sense, apparently independent of any logical and critical evaluation, that the idea is right or wrong. There is no unanimity of opinion on how intuition operates, but we bring to any moment the backlog of our prior experience and knowledge. New information is filtered by that backlog, and the process does not always take place at the conscious level in such a way that it can be immediately observed by the thinker and articulated. Thus something may well strike us as correct or incorrect and only further reflection will allow us to consciously and logically identify the basis for our initial response. It is possible that this is the process by which we intuit.

It is also possible to know truth by faith or on the basis of trust. We can arrive at a knowledge of truth by accepting the testimony of someone who knows the truth about a matter. Much education is based on this method. We know that certain things are true not because we have determined for ourselves, either empirically or logically, that they are true, but because we accept the testimony of a teacher or parent or scholar or other trusted authority. Often the teacher bases his or her judgment on the authority of others as well. Much of the study of history is the result of this method: we accept the testimony of others with respect to what some ancient figure said or did.[7] Certainly this method of knowing truth is more efficient than trying to discover everything ourselves, and it makes available to us material from the past that we could never recover for ourselves.

While this method is a valid means of knowing truth, it obviously has a weakness. The truth content of what we know by faith is no better than the knowledge and integrity of our authority. Or to put it in different terms, trusting in the testimony of someone who is not trustworthy will give us faulty knowledge. This information must by critically and carefully received when it comes from finite and fallen human beings.

Faith plays a particularly significant role in the knowledge of the believer. The information in inspired Scripture, while mediated through human authors, claims to have its ultimate origins with God. Thus it gives us knowledge about matters that could not be known apart from such disclosure. In addition, it comes from the omniscient God himself whose knowledge and experience are not limited as human knowledge and experience are. God is able to see the totality of reality and knows how all its components are related. Scripture contains not only data as to what happened at various points in history (e.g., the Creation, the Fall, the Exodus, the Resurrection), it also provides us with an inspired interpretation of the meaning of many of the events it reports. Thus Scripture becomes a unique and significant source of knowledge for the believer. The knowledge contained in the Bible is received through faith, and we accept that truth on the basis of trust in authority.[8] This does not mean, however, that we approach it superficially and uncritically; though we must always fully stand under its authority—but more about that later.

In practice our knowledge usually does not come purely through any one of the above methods but involves several methods operating together.[9]

Questions For Further Consideration:

1. Can you identify beliefs to which you are committed or values that you hold on the basis of knowledge that has come as a result of: (a) empiricism, (b) reason, (c) intuition, (d) faith?

2. Can you think of a situation where you had to change your understanding about something because you realized that the observations and experiences of others were more accurate than yours?

3. Can you recall a time when your understanding was changed on the basis of faith?

4. Have you ever made the same mistake as the blind men in the story did? What caused you to realize that there was more to reality than what you had first supposed?

5. Have you ever been in a situation where you failed to recognize important data because you were looking for something else or where personal interest caused you to miss something that in hindsight proved to be of great significance?

Notes

[1]At the popular level, people often fail to distinguish between data and interpretation as they make observations, reach conclusions, and assimilate them into their worldview. Many major differences of opinion result from a failure to differentiate between the facts we know and our interpretation of that data (i.e., what the data means and how it relates to other things we know). Proverbs 18:17 says, "The first to plead his case seems just, Until another comes and examines him." Certainly

the proverb emphasizes the importance of getting all the information possible before making up one's mind. It may, as well, recognize the reality of dissenting interpretations of the data and stand as an exhortation to consider other ways of looking at the facts before reaching a conclusion.

2David Wolfe, *Epistemology: The Justification of Belief* (InterVarsity Press, 1982), p. 48.

3McMinn and Foster (*Christians in the Crossfire* [Newberg, Oregon: The Barclay Press, 1990], p. 42) point out that people are often guilty of what they call the "correlation error," that is, confusing causation with correlation. Just because two things occur together does not mean that one was caused by the other. People regularly blame the problems of poor performance by students in the public schools on inadequate funding, poor teachers, educrats, etc., and while it is easy to establish a correlation between poor results on standardized tests and one or another of those factors, establishing a cause effect relationship is much more difficult.

4Wolfe (*Epistemology*, p. 33) cites Kekulé's discovery of the molecular structure of benzene as an example; Montgomery ("The Theologian's Craft," *Concordia Theological Monthly* 37 [1966], 71) notes the example of Crick and Watson's discovery of the structure of the DNA molecule.

5L. J. Henderson, "Hippocrates and the Practice of Medicine," in *The Practical Cogitator*, p. 289.

6For these points I am indebted to my colleague, Dr. Delbert Hanson. This would not be true of the scientific breakthroughs arrived at through intuition. The scientists who were convinced of the correctness of an idea that "just came to them" carefully tested the idea to determine its validity before they ever presented it to the community for consideration. One would imagine that they tested it even more carefully than they might otherwise since the scientific community is not especially receptive to the argument that the scientist "just knows" the theory is right or that he knows it is right because it came to him in a vision.

7Again I am indebted to Del Hanson for this example.

8Berkhof (*Systematic Theology* [Eerdmans, 1941], p. 501) says, "Christian faith...is man's persuasion of the truth of Scripture on the basis of the authority of God." He also points out (pp. 493-94) that in classical Greek the words translated *faith* or *to believe* "meant a conviction based on confidence in a person and in his testimony, which is distinguished from knowledge based on personal investigation." The same is true of faith in the Old Testament. According to Speiser (*Genesis*, Anchor Bible [Doubleday, 1964], p. 112), "The invariable translation of Heb. he'emin as 'believed' does not always do justice to the original. The basic sense of the form is 'to affirm, recognize as valid.'"

[9]Note, for example, Montgomery's discussion of the way scientific theories are formed ("Theologian's Craft," pp. 72-75). See also the discussion by Belenky and others in *Women's Ways of Knowing*, Basic Books, 1973. Note especially chapter 7, "Constructed Knowledge: Integrating the Voices."

CHAPTER 2

Worldview And The Importance Of Assumptions

From one perspective our task appears to be to learn as much as we possibly can about as many areas of knowledge as possible and then to put that information together into a coherent and somewhat comprehensive model of reality. Both education and experience acquaint us with different areas of knowledge, allowing us to become familiar with various specialties, like European history, carpentry, or theology. But there is another dimension to knowing, one which is crucial in gaining a better understanding of reality. As David Wolfe[1] points out, every person at any point in life has a belief system or worldview that provides orientation and seeks to make sense out of experience and reality. He compares this interpretive framework to a spider web. While there are elements near the edge in the worldview that are held at a level that amounts to little more than casual opinion not strongly adhered to, toward the center of the web are other beliefs and values that give structure and coherence to the system. Included among these core beliefs are the fundamental values and nonnegotiable commitments of an individual. The ideas that we consider the most certain, and to which we are most deeply committed, are sometimes called *control beliefs*[G] because of the way they function in interpreting experience and in determining our responses to the circumstances that confront us.

The components of this belief system come from a variety of sources. Some are arrived at through observation or experience, while others are the result of tradition, parents' teaching, or the teaching of some authority outside the family. Some components seem to be the result of such long-term exposure to certain ideas and values that we finally accept them as true—often without ever evaluating them.[2] This can pose a serious danger to the Christian, who can easily gravitate into living according to non-Christian, or even anti-Christian beliefs, without realizing it. As Wolfe notes, however,

> Normally our beliefs come to us in a rather undeveloped form, and we elaborate on them and seek to understand their implications as we make them more our own. The important issue epistemologically is whether we are warranted in believing a particular scheme....The question of warrant with respect to a given interpretive scheme[G] is answered by a thorough examination of the scheme....It is answered by casting one's beliefs on the rock of criticism and by seeing...how well they fare. By such a process of testing it is possible to show that one is (or discover that one is not) warranted in what may be a subjectively arrived at and personally important belief system.[3]

Wolfe[4] argues that the entire interpretive scheme produced by a person's worldview should meet certain requirements. First, the various elements in the system must be consistent with one another; if there are contradictions among the principles, there is a problem somewhere in the system. Second, not only must the principles not conflict with one another, they must cohere and allow us to trace relationships between various parts of experience.[5] Third, our belief system should be as comprehensive as possible. Fourth, it should be able to account not only for man's positive characteristics but also for his fallenness; it must be able to address both God's sovereignty and man's responsible choice; it must be able to account not only for the judgment of the wicked but also for the suffering of the righteous.[6] Finally, our belief system should be congruent with experience. Often several explanations will account for what happens without either internal contradictions or conflict with our control beliefs[G], but certain possible interpretations seem to us (perhaps primarily because they are closer to our personal experiences) to be more consistent with the experiences that they cover.[7]

We inevitably begin with a belief system, and our task is to continually test it against the totality of our experience.[8] As experience interacts with our belief system, we interpret experience on the basis of that belief system. At the same time the data of experience impacts our belief system and refines it. In some instances we will be confronted by portions of reality that are totally new to us and that we did not know existed. This new information and experience will be interpreted by the belief system but at the same time will sometimes require a modification of the worldview to accommodate the new data. New information and our belief system constantly interact, with each influencing the other.

Sometimes we will be confronted by data that calls certain aspects of our belief system into question. In some instances we can simply allow the problematic data to co-exist in tension with our belief system as we wait for additional information that will finally allow us to see how the once problematic material is compatible with our belief system. On other occasions, the new data will require changes in parts of our belief system, parts that are not warranted because they are not in keeping with the facts[9] of experience and thus cannot withstand the critical scrutiny that the new data requires. Usually the required modifications involve elements near the edges of the web of the belief system, but sometimes the gap between worldview and the data we are confronted with is so great that more fundamental changes are required. The gap can sometimes be so great that a person is forced to discard the entire belief system to which they have been committed. Such experiences can be quite traumatic and as Walsh notes, "as the worldview suffers collapse, the entire world seems to come crashing down with it."[10] In such situations the person is often open to conversion from one worldview to another.[11]

The tension between our worldview and experience sometimes produces less constructive responses as well. In some instances people become somewhat schizophrenic in that they operate from one worldview in their profession and from a very different one at church or in other areas of life. Sometimes people respond with what Walsh calls *entrenchment*, in which people "tend to dig in their heels and hang on to what they've got, a survivalist mentality emerges, and we witness a culture-wide recommitment to the very world view and the very faith that seems to be discredited by one's historical reality."[12] These responses do not contribute to growth in thinking as Christians. But in any case, the constant interaction between the data of experience and our belief system is essential (and will happen regardless of whether we want it to) because it both refines our understanding of reality and demonstrates the validity of the belief system. Wolfe says,

> Only to the extent that a scheme remains open to continued testing is it able to display its credentials. Only then can it show the strength of its internal structure and its ability to illuminate experience. Far from being a favor, to protect one's interpretive scheme from criticism is to rob it of the only way it can display its claims to truth.[13]

Being confronted also helps us to understand our belief system — we are pushed to think through why we believe as we do. Thus the Christian should welcome exposure to new ideas and facts; he or she should delight in finding out how different cultures view things and rejoice in gaining insight into human experience. This continual process of learning can be entered into through great literature, through discovering how people respond to various traumatic experiences or how societies operate. Understanding can be expanded by finding out how great civilizations in the past lived and why they declined; it can be broadened through knowledge about how people learn or even how plants grow. Christians should deliberately seek exposure to great art and music to expand the boundaries of their own experience and thinking. The experiences and learning interact with the belief system that is in place and both test its validity to interpret and organize the new data and refine and expand its limits. This can lead to additional dimensions in our belief system. Pushing ourselves to new frontiers is part of the fascination of life.

The Sources Of Data For Christian Thinking

The data from which we draw information for the process we have described comes from the totality of reality. Since our goal is *Christian* thinking, it seems useful to identify our sources of information in terms of two theological categories — general and special revelation[G]. We will discuss the two sources in more detail later, but for now a general description seems in order. We live in the world and obviously that world is an important part of the reality that we seek to understand. Christians affirm that the world has been created by God and that he has revealed something of himself to all people in the created world — thus the term general revelation[G]. At the same time the believing community has recognized that God has revealed himself in a special way to his people. The means of special revelation is varied as Hebrews 1:1 makes clear and involves both the communication of information and intrusions into the historical process (e.g., the Exodus; the Resurrection, etc.). We have a repository of that special revelation in Scripture, and thus the believer must include that important source in his attempt to understand reality.

Because the Bible is such an important source of truth for the believer, it is very easy to suppose that everything he or she really needs to know can be found in Scripture, but as Arthur Holmes points out, "Revelation is not a source of information about everything. It is the Christian's 'final and sufficient rule for faith and practice,' but it is not exhaustive, even on matters of doctrine and morality, let alone on other subjects."[14] To segregate the biblical perspective from everything else that can be learned about most topics is like looking at a scene in a room through a keyhole or trying to get the whole picture of what is happening on a football field by looking through powerful binoculars with a narrow field-of-view. The limited perspective will often leave us with an incomplete and sometimes distorted picture of the reality that is there, leading us to false conclusions about the truth.

The Christian's task involves identifying and integrating all the relevant data from both general and special revelation. Clearly the task is one that will never be fully accomplished. We are finite creatures trying to understand a highly complex world created by an infinite God and inhabited by complex human beings made in God's image. To suppose that we can understand every detail of reality and the way all the details fit together is absurd. We will always be left with conflicts and tensions and inconsistencies. We can, though, make progress and that progress will move us closer to maturity and the ability to think Christianly about life and our world.

As we noted above, every person has a basic set of assumptions, a *worldview*, a perspective, which allows for the organizing and explaining of various events and ideas encountered in the world. We take the components of our worldview from many different sources. We are influenced by what we are taught both formally and informally, by the various authority figures we meet, by the media, by our experiences on the job, by our hobbies, and by the other experiences of life in general. We are imprinted cognitively, emotionally and relationally by all of our experiences; everything that impacts us as human beings living in the world has the potential for contributing in some way to our worldview. These influences and the ways they impact us, both consciously and subconsciously are extremely complex, and (as might be expected) the influences are neither coherent nor necessarily accurate. Because the data we receive are so varied, we are tempted to keep various spheres of life segregated rather than to integrate all the relevant data into a unified scheme.

We are like the neighborhood grocer who receives shipments from different suppliers: canned goods from one, fresh produce from another, bottled drinks from yet another, and meats from still another. All find their proper place in the store according to the supplier, until the man who supplies fresh produce begins providing bottled juices, which overlap with bottled drinks. Then the meat supplier comes out with a line of canned meats, competing with similar items brought in by the canned goods supplier. As things become more complex, the grocer begins to feel the need of a more comprehensive store-plan, a basic overall pattern of placement that will provide an appropriate shelf space for every grocery item, no matter which supplier brought it. Like the grocer, we need a comprehensive plan, a unified mind that organizes all the data of observation and experience coherently in our minds.

As David Gill points out, however, the fragmented nature of life in our time makes it very difficult to develop a unified mind. In his words, "The sheer speed and the overwhelming volume of information to be mastered, the competitiveness of the university, workplace and marketplace...take their toll on us and keep us from grasping the whole of life."[15] He further notes the role of the modern university in contributing to this fragmentation:

> Factually and technically, today's universities offer extraor-dinary possibilities for knowledge and specialized expertise. The university-trained parts of our minds can be extremely muscular and potent. For several reasons, however, such intellectual muscle has little in common with wisdom, moral

depth, or spiritual sensitivity and understanding. In one sense today's universities pose a threat to society by arming graduates with powerful tools — but without the holistic wisdom and character necessary to employ these powers in the best interests of themselves, their neighbors or God.[16]

Thus it often happens that a person by virtue of education or profession or special area of interest is quite well versed in and has an excellent grasp of reality in one sphere, while at the same time that individual's awareness of other areas is superficial and unsophisticated.[17] A danger that must be avoided if we are to develop a worldview that is consistent with reality is a kind of thinking where we reduce complex issues to simple ones (something commonly referred to as *reductionism*[G]).[18] A related danger lies in assuming that our experiences and observations are the same as everyone else's. We suppose that our experiences with the public schools or with our kids or with the church or with the medical doctors or with lawyers or with other people allow us to reach accurate conclusions about the larger reality. We also assume that others have these or similar experiences, and such assumptions often result in confusion and frustration when others don't understand us and don't agree with us.

Cultural factors are another avenue through which we receive contributions to our worldview, and Kraft defines worldview as "the central systematization of conceptions of reality to which the members of the culture assent (largely unconsciously) and from which stems their value system."[19] As Phillips and Brown note, "A particular worldview thus pervades a culture and is passed on to succeeding generations as a 'social inheritance.'"[20] We are immersed in a culture and are constantly exposed to the ideas and values to which our culture assents. We absorb many of those values and ways of doing things, and the environment in which we live "gives us the impression that our way of doing things is 'the right way to behave,'...instill[ing] within us an overwhelming sense that our outlook is the 'right way to believe.'"[21] Many of these ideas are part of what some refer to as the zeitgeist[G] of the culture. This term refers to "the general intellectual, moral, and cultural climate of an era,"[22] and these ideas are regularly reinforced at both the conscious and the subconscious levels by the frequency with which they occur throughout the culture. We are bombarded with certain ideas and values and the constant repetition causes those ideas to be set into our worldview as givens.

Hearing an idea — even if it is wrong — presented as the truth over a long period of time often results in the acceptance of the idea as true, particularly when the source is one to which we have attributed authority status. The idea will remain as an important element in the interpretive grid as long as there is no careful, critical thinking about the issue and little in our experience to challenge the view. Western culture's acceptance of individualism as a higher value than community responsibility is one example of this. The priority of human rights and the idea that all people are created equal are others that many people throughout the world and at other times in history would see very differently. These values, by virtue of their constant repetition, are assumed to be valid and rarely does anyone question the values. We simply assume that they are true because we have heard them expressed as truth so frequently throughout our lives.

Many groups use this principle to promote their particular agendas. I often encounter students or people in churches who have been told for years that a certain thing was true, which they take as unassailable evidence that they should accept the idea as a fact, when even a casual examination of the biblical data (or sometimes experience from life) makes it apparent that the concept is much less certain than they suppose. Many racial and gender stereotypes come into worldviews in this way. The modern media also have great power in shaping worldview. They often promote their own agenda by selectively presenting those stories and ideas that further the point they want to make and then simply repeating the same ideas over and over as truth. Few people go to the trouble to look critically at the issues and the evidence, and the idea becomes established as the truth in the minds of many people. Sometimes teachers or politicians or leaders effectively promote a particular agenda by selectively communicating only the information that supports their agenda. The regular repetition of the information then sets it into the worldview of those whose exposure is limited to that group.

Numerous examples of this could be given. Certainly those groups advocating the victim status of various groups of people are often guilty of this as are denominations who focus on their particular doctrinal agenda to the neglect of the biblical balance.

Fringe groups like those who deny the Holocaust or groups that see government conspiracies at every turn are able to keep their aberrant views going by repeating certain anecdotes over and over to their followers while at the same time encouraging (or sometimes demanding) that their adherents avoid listening to other sources of information that would present another side of the issue. McMinn and Foster refer to this phenomenon as *groupthink,* in which members of a group value agreement to such a degree that the members "become so cohesive and the members so protective of the group and the group leader, that differing points of view are actively discouraged."[23]

There are numerous other ways that our environment can impact us and give us a distorted picture of reality. McMinn and Foster point out the power of vivid images to impact and per-suade. As they say, "Vivid illustrations tend to overwhelm us and capture more than just our imagination. Responding to such illustrations, we often ignore the big picture and focus on the features of a specific case"[24] which may not be representative of the larger reality. A good *dog story* has a powerful impact on most people whether the point it makes is true or not. The image of dying children in some third world country has a far greater impact in convincing people to give their money to a certain cause than simple information about the needs in that part of the world ever could. At the same time people aware of the impact of touching anecdotes and carefully selected stories and images can easily mislead people and manipulate worldview and people's understanding of reality. The impression registers in a person's mind sometimes without that individual being fully aware of the impact it has made. In speaking of such uncon-sciously influenced people, Leland Ryken has noted,

> To regard their world view as being solely the domain of theoretical thought is to invite unawareness about them-selves. People may assent to the proposition that the true end in life is not to make money and accumulate possessions, but if their minds are filled with images of big houses and fancy clothes, their actual behavior will run in the direction of materialism. People may theoretically believe in the ideal of chastity and faithful wedded love, but if their minds are filled with images of exposed bodies and songs of seduction,

their sexual behavior will have a large admixture of lust and sexual license in it.

Unless we recognize the powerful role of images in a world view, our world view and the behavior it produces will continue to be the muddled things they often are. We also need to recognize that the quality of our life and character is heavily affected by the quality of the images that we habitually take into our minds and imaginations.[25]

Art, literature, and music have an extraordinary power to evoke emotional responses and to make an important connection with a person's previous experience, wielding a doubly powerful potential for persuasion. The modern media's ability to combine the informative and the emotional in music and film affords an extremely powerful tool for influencing people's worldview, particularly when those messages are repeated regularly or presented in such a way as to keep them flitting through a person's mind. While many advertising executives would argue that the images in television commercials do not influence viewer's behavior, they budget millions of dollars to such advertising. Such expensive actions speak far louder than their words of denial. Clearly, images, especially when vivid and repeated, influence behavior. And it is difficult to see how one's behavior can be changed without a change in character.[26] The positive use of this technique is reflected in the emphasis that the Bible places on meditation; regular reflection on God's truth is an important mechanism for internalizing the principles in such a way that they begin to affect attitudes, behavior, and ultimately character.

Popular opinion about a controversial issue can sometimes be changed by the skillful use of emotion-evoking communication techniques. Public opinion about issues like abortion, homosexuality, civil rights, women's rights, welfare, and so on can be impacted in a major way by the media. An article in the *Orange County (CA) Register* (Feb. 6, 1995) quotes actress Glenn Close about her role in a recent television movie in which she played a high-ranking army officer discharged from the military because of her sexual orientation. "This is the kind of story that belongs on television because I want it to reach as many people as possible and reach them in their homes among their loved ones. I hope it will get people talking. I hope it will change opinions....I

seek out the kinds of stories, like this, that will educate them."
Depicting these kinds of relationships positively and in a touching and compassionate way while at the same time provoking
the emotion that unjust treatment generates makes a significant
impact on people and does it in a way that does not stimulate
critical thinking about the issue. Persistent exposure to these
messages often results in worldview changes, without the holder
of the worldview even being aware of the changes.

Worldview is often decisive in determining how we see and
interpret the information and experiences of life. A recent newspaper editorial recognized the importance of assumptions in
determining conclusions. The article said,

> Reassessments about public policy forced by political reality
> are better than no reassessment at all. But it is seldom the
> case, when looking at public policies, that the facts really
> speak for themselves. People with different underlying
> assumptions about what constitutes a good society can look
> at the same set of facts and come to radically different con-
> clusions about what their implications are.[27]

Brown and Phillips say,

> Metaphysical arguments usually end up where they begin.
> An atheist will take the evidence of the world order and con-
> clude that God, in fact, does not exist. Using the same evi-
> dence, theists conclude that God does exist. One's
> assumptions determine the outcome of his arguments.[28]

Clearly, assumptions are vitally important, and assumptions are
largely the result of worldview, making worldview equally
important.

Christians are certainly not immune to this influence, and it
can be seen in almost every area of life including the interpretation of texts, even biblical texts. Stan Gundry examined the way
biblical prophecy about the end times (the part of theology
known as eschatology) has been interpreted, concluding that
"factors other than purely exegetical and theological considerations have been more influential in the history of eschatology
than we would care to admit."[29] He found a parallel between the
changing emphases in eschatology and prominent themes in the

zeitgeist of the time. The correlation that he found led him to conclude, "I have presented enough to suggest that we as Christian exegetes and theologians are susceptible to influences from the moods and conditions of our times, and especially so in our eschatologies."[30] Linda Mercadante reached a similar conclusion in her study of how biblical passages dealing with women's roles in the church have been interpreted over the years. She says, "By setting each writer's interpretation in the context of his or her socio-historical time, we can see that the interpreters were, and are, affected by their age."[31] She further notes that "These effects have not only come in accommodation to the spirit of their age — the charge often leveled at more 'liberal' scholars by more conservative ones — but the effects can also be seen in an almost reflex action against the spirit of the age."[32] The examples presented by Mercadante reveal a pattern.

> At first...in spite of the radical changes occurring in society all around them, the theologians fail to make mention of them...After a "time-lag" which seemed to last several decades at least, the first real responses were almost uniformly negative and condemnatory. The odd thing, however, is that many of the changes so vociferously decried by one generation of theologians and church leaders...became the very changes adopted into the churches of their theological descendants.[33]

The impact of the zeitgeist[G] takes place both at the popular and at the scholarly level. For example, opinions about women and their appropriate roles have changed radically over the past two centuries, and those changes in the zeitgeist are reflected at every level. As women's roles in society have expanded and as they have been given greater educational opportunities, opinions about their roles have changed. Many of the opinions expressed a century ago — opinions fully consistent with the spirit of the age in which they were expressed — now do not seem convincing, given the current zeitgeist. The Old Testament book of Song of Songs describes the woman as taking the initiative in various aspects of the relationship depicted there, including the couple's love making. Ginsburg notes that some 19th century commentators took the aggressiveness of the woman as proof that the book was an allegory[G] rather than a description of a real relationship between a man and a woman.[34] Such an argument would carry little persuasive weight today. The same contrast is sometimes seen in literature and art. As Bernard Holland points out, the changing values of society make it difficult today to perform certain plays (e.g., *The Taming of the Shrew*) or operas (some of Wagner's works) because modern sensibilities are strongly offended by material reflecting, according to Holland, "simply the way most people thought"[35] when the piece was written.

Often the influence of the zeitgeist is positive, and an ongoing dialogue with the world is essential. Often the *world* recognizes societal problems and discovers truth in the natural realm before the Christian community does, and as Mercadante notes above, it sometimes takes a while before Christians are willing to acknowledge that truth. Certainly concerns about the environment, civil rights, and gender equity did not always have their origins in the Christian community. The dialogue with the world is critical for the believing community.

But at the same time Christians must be careful not to be influenced by the spirit of the age in such a way that they assimilate the world's values and allow them to replace biblical ones. We live in a world where the environment of ideas is not wholly integrated and where it is not always easy to discover exactly what the contradictions are. The difficulty in determining which elements of our environment are good and which are bad is captured in Kidner's comment about the power of God's Word to deliver us from hidden faults (Ps. 19:12). He says, "A fault may be hidden not because it is too small to see, but because it is too characteristic to register."[36] Our conversation with the world must proceed carefully and critically as we seek to learn the truth that people made in the image of God are pointing out to us, while at the same time not absorbing distorted depictions of reality from our culture and world. In any culture there will be elements that are true, those that are false (given human finiteness and fallenness), and many that are neither true nor false, but that simply reflect different ways of looking at things. As an example of the last, many different ways of greeting one another or classifying animals or colors and many social customs are neither right nor wrong. We often gain valuable insights into the nature of reality through an awareness of how other people view these things.

There are, of course, many possible worldviews and it is not the purpose of this work to describe even the major ones.[37] One of the interesting and challenging things about living in the 20th-century West is that we live in a world that is pluralistic to a degree that is unprecedented in history, inundated as we are with ideas from so many worldviews. At the same time there are certain currents of the zeitgeist that have influenced, and continue to strongly influence perceptions of reality. Two movements/philosophies, modernity and postmodernism[G], have had a particularly powerful influence on modern Western culture, and in the next two chapters we want to consider some of their primary characteristics and the ways they have impacted thought and practice.

As we have suggested, our task is made more difficult and challenging by the fact that we live in a pluralistic world where we are influenced by many different worldviews, and our situation is much like the neighborhood grocer mentioned earlier in the chapter. We may be taking a class in literature or education where the assumptions of postmodernism are the prevailing ones; during the same semester we may be taking a science class where the assumptions of modernity dominate. In the workplace there may be a subtle mixture of assumptions, and then we are powerfully impacted by movies and books and music, reflecting any number of worldviews. It becomes difficult in such a world to forge out a coherent and biblically informed worldview, but the dangers in failing to do so make it imperative that we try.

Questions For Further Consideration:

1. Identify at least five values (components of your belief system) to which you are committed because you are a Christian.

2. Identify some values to which you are committed because of each of the following: parents, education, influence of friends, experience, the Bible, church.

3. Can you think of a time when experience created a major tension with values to which you were committed? Have you ever been in a situation where your experience seemed to create ten-

sion with what you had been taught in church? How was the tension resolved?

4. Can you think of a time when your worldview changed? What caused the change? How did you feel as you were struggling with the tension that forced you to rethink some values that you believed were true?

5. What can you do to identify and counteract the negative effects of the media and the world in general on your world-view? Can you think of a time when so-called secular influences helped to bring better understanding and balance to your worldview? Can you think of a time when you realized that these influences were hindering your efforts at effective Christian thinking and behavior?

Notes

[1]Wolfe, pp. 44-69.

[2]This is apparently one of Paul's concerns in Romans 12:1-3. He recognizes the subtle and effective way the world's values are assimilated by the Christian and he warns us to be on guard. A similar warning is contained in Proverbs 4:20-27. For a very helpful discussion of the danger and how to avoid succumbing to the problem of worldliness (as the Bible views the problem), see Eugene Peterson, *A Long Obedience in the Same Direction*, InterVarsity Press, 1980, pp. 11-17.

[3]Wolfe, p. 56.

[4]*Ibid.*, pp. 52-55.

[5]As Wolfe points out, a long list of randomly chosen names might not contain contradictions, but it might not be coherent in that the names provide no basis for relating components of experience together in a meaningful way.

[6]Job's friends, for example, were able to deal very well with the judgment of the wicked, but they had no place in their system for the suffering of righteous people. Their system did not allow that as a possibility, but such suffering is a part of reality.

[7]The present author wrote a commentary on Song of Songs

(*Bible Study Commentary* [Grand Rapids, Michigan, 1988]), a book about which there is perhaps more difference of opinion than any other book in the Bible. The following comment by Jack Deere (unpublished Th.D. dissertation, Dallas Theological Seminary, 1984, p. 2) appropriately describes the way a preferred interpretation of Song of Songs (and many other and theological ideas as well) must be set forth. Deere says, "This particular reading of the Song is offered as one among several that are plausible and defensible from the text itself without unduly 'straining' the meaning of the text or 'reading into' the text what is not there." The interpretation presented in the present author's commentary was chosen out of several that can be defended as "correct" because it seemed to be the most congruent with the data of the text and experience.

[8]By experience we do not just mean the things that happen to us; rather, we are speaking of everything to which we are exposed. It will include what we are taught, both formally and informally, what we think about, what we hear from authority figures, what we are exposed to through the media, what we experience as we function in a profession, and so on. It will also include those things that impact us emotionally and subconsciously. It will include everything that impacts us as human beings living in the world regardless of whether the initiative for the factor was internal or external.

[9]It must be noted here that *facts* are rather elusive and what scholars present as facts sometimes turn out to be different than the claims attached to them. For example, the *fact* of a flat earth turned out to be incorrect. Often what the various academic disciplines present as facts are so influenced by questionable presuppositions that the so-called fact falls quite short of certainty. Clearly part of the task of Christian thinking is to carefully test the data with which we are confronted in order to determine when we are dealing with genuine facts and when we are dealing with interpretations or partial understandings of reality.

[10]Brian Walsh, "Worldviews, Modernity and the Task of Christian College Education," *Faculty Dialogue* 18 (1992), p. 23.

[11]*Ibid.* It is sometimes the case that dissonance between worldview and experience is used by God to bring people to

faith. Conversion to Christianity brings about a radical worldview change that includes changes in core beliefs.

[12]Walsh, p. 24. McMinn and Foster (pp. 43-44) cite the example of a woman who claimed to receive messages from aliens from outer space and gained a group of followers. She indicated that the aliens would come on a certain date to take the "faithful" away. When the date passed with no sign of the space creatures, the group concluded that the earth had been spared because of the faithfulness of their group. Self-justification often plays a role in the entrenchment response.

[13]Wolfe, p. 65.

[14] Arthur Holmes, *All Truth is God's Truth*, p. 77.

[15]David Gill, *The Opening of the Christian Mind* (Downers Grove, Illinois: InterVarsity Press, 1989), p. 23.

[16]*Ibid.*, p. 47.

[17]One is reminded of the remark attributed to Will Rogers, "We are all ignorant, just in different subjects."

[18]My colleague Dr. John Ingram refers to this kind of thinking as "nothing buttery." We suppose that good emotional health involves *nothing but* a good relationship with God, or we suppose that a good marriage involves *nothing but* fidelity or commitment or that good parenting involves *nothing but* loving one's kids.

[19]Kraft, *Christianity in Culture*, p. 53.

[20]Phillips and Brown, *Making Sense of Your World*, p. 34.

[21]Brown and Phillips, p. 35.

[22]*Webster's Ninth New Collegiate Dictionary*, 1986.

[23]McMinn and Foster, *Christians in the Crossfire*, p. 174.

[24]*Ibid.*, p. 38.

[25]Leland Ryken, "The Creative Arts," in *The Making of the Christian Mind*, ed. Arthur Holmes, p. 106.

[26]The idea is expressed well in the old saying, "Sow a thought, reap a deed; sow a deed, reap a habit; sow a habit, reap a character."

[27]*Orange County (CA) Register*, March 1, 1995.

[28]Brown and Phillips, *Making Sense of Your World*, p. 75. The role of assumptions and worldview in influencing conclusions will be discussed further in the chapter on general revelation.

[29]Stanley Gundry, "Hermeneutics or _Zeitgeist_ as the Determining Factor in the History of Eschatologies," _Journal of the Evangelical Theological Society_, 20 (1977), 50.

[30]_Ibid._, p. 55.

[31]Linda Mercadante, "The Male-Female Debate: Can We Read the Bible Objectively?," _Crux_ 15 (1979), 21.

[32]_Ibid._

[33]_Ibid._

[34]C. D. Ginsburg, _The Song of Songs and Coheleth_ (New York: KTAV, reprinted, 1970), p. 105. Ginsburg notes the argument of Dr. Bennett (_Congregational Magazine_, 1838, pp. 148-49) who took the woman's "solicitous seeking after him" and "her praises of his person" as proof that this is not a human love song. Bennett argued that the woman's role in the Song could not be accounted for on the basis of cultural differences between the Near East and the West. He said, "It would be more abhorrent from the secluded, submissive character of Eastern brides to ask the gentleman to come and kiss them, than it would be from the dignified confidence of British women. It is not, according to Bennett, a question of climate or of age, but of nature." He says, "Till fishes mount to sing with larks on the shady boughs, and nightingales dive to ocean depths to court the whales, no man, of any age, of any clime, of any rank, can be supposed to write ordinary love songs in such a style."

[35]Bernard Holland, "Wagner Suffers in Outliving his Era," _The Orange County Register_, September 4, 1994. Show, p. 31. The article was originally written for _The New York Times_.

[36]Derek Kidner, _Psalms 1-72_, Tyndale Old Testament Commentary (Downers Grove, Illinois: InterVarsity Press, 1973), p. 100.

[37]For an excellent introductory discussion of a number of the major belief systems see James D. Sire, _The Universe Next Door_ (Downers Grove, Illinois: InterVarsity Press, 1976). See also Phillips and Brown, _Making Sense of Your World_, pp. 41-67.

CHAPTER 3

Modernity And The Challenge To Christian Thinking

The movement commonly referred to as modernity has many of its roots in the Enlightenment of the 17th and 18th centuries. According to Thomas Oden, "Modernity is less a time than a conceptual place, an ideological tone. It is less a distinct period than an attitude. Although it has had many premodern[G] manifestations, it was not until the 19th century that [modernity] began to expand from the pockets of the intelligentsia into general circulation in Western society."[1]

Arthur Shapiro says that, "The history of Western civilization since the Middle Ages is commonly, and reasonably, portrayed as the retreat of faith in the face of reason."[2] Such an observation reflects a history in which conflicts between the church and people like Galileo and Copernicus were again and again decided in favor of human observation rather than the pronouncements made by theological authorities. As a result of such encounters it became increasingly evident "that man was competent, by reason and the evidence provided by his senses, to discover his own truth,"[3] and often that truth seemed to be at variance with what the church was teaching. Since an important function of religion had been to explain those phenomena that could not be explained on the basis of cause and effect, each new discovery had the effect of reducing the explanatory function of religion, and therefore (in appearance at least) its power; to many it appeared that the need for God was reduced as well.[4] In view of the pattern that was emerging, it seemed to many that human reason, coupled with a careful study of the world, could provide an explanation for everything in the physical world. The result was a world that was more and more secularized.

René Descartes and Francis Bacon contributed significantly to this process. Bacon emphasized the importance of experiment and empirical[G] evidence as the "route to understanding nature's secrets and attaining a genuine scientific knowledge."[5] Descartes wanted to find a solid foundation for intellectual activity in general, "to establish irrefutable arguments and unshakable evidence for the truth."[6] Descartes concluded that the resources of the human mind are adequate for this task in ways that institutions and traditions could not be. Descartes' methodology, emphasizing a mathematically based and more abstract reasoning, further contributed to the confidence in human reasoning that seemed to be reflected in the great advances being made in the sciences. According to Walker,

> This natural philosophy (science), and the methodology of Francis Bacon (1561-1626) and René Descartes (1596-1650), [seemed] to suggest that the world was not run by divine decree but by natural laws; laws that can be discovered by the application of the human mind through the senses (by observation) to the physical world. The world—and especially the empirical...world—[became] the prime focus of attention.[7]

The emphasis on the importance of human reason, and the desire to achieve certainty in intellectual pursuits, shifted attention away from theological speculation, while the traditions and understandings of the past (including those found in the teachings of the church and Scripture) were devalued and replaced by the assured results of science and philosophy.[8] As Harvey notes,

> Enlightenment thought...embraced the idea of progress, and actively sought that break with history and tradition which modernity espouses. It was, above all, a secular movement that sought the demystification and desacralization of knowledge and social organizations in order to liberate human beings from their chains....Doctrines of equality, liberty, faith in human intelligence (once allowed the benefits of education), and universal reason abounded.[9]

Out of these ideas emerged what many refer to as the *Enlightenment project*. According to Harvey,

That project amounted to an extraordinary intellectual effort on the part of Enlightenment thinkers "to develop objective science, universal morality and law, and autonomous art according to their inner logic." The idea was to use the accumulation of knowledge generated by many individuals working freely and creatively for the pursuit of human emancipation and the enrichment of daily life. The scientific domination of nature promised freedom from scarcity, want, and the arbitrariness of human calamity. The development of rational forms of social organization and rational modes of thought promised liberation from the irrationalities of myth, religion, superstition, release from the arbitrary use of power as well as from the dark side of our own human natures.[10]

Three Characteristics Of Modernity

Three of the classic characteristics of modernity have greatly impacted worldview over the past century. First, the **primacy of human reason and the ability of humans to discover and communicate truth** is an important given of modernity. Since the ability to verify the truth empirically is generally limited to studies of the physical world, the result is the elevation of the physical sciences to the neglect of the more intuitive disciplines. Related to this is an intense suspicion of tradition, in part because previous generations were not trained in modern methodologies and were thus unable to think and observe as critically and carefully as modern scholars. (As many have pointed out, this attitude often borders on arrogance and can be characterized as intellectual snobbery.) Great advances in science and technology have contributed to the confidence and value given to the scientific disciplines in the public perception. As Shapiro points out there is a pragmatic dimension to the confidence that people generally have in science. "The public accepts and daily uses the fruits of physical science; it knows that the internal combustion engine and the measles vaccine were not derived from the study of Holy Writ."[11]

Modernity is also characterized by a second belief, **that both our understanding and our society are continually progressing.**[12] The growth in understanding and knowledge that is evident in human history contributes to this progress and presumably guarantees it, and the great advances made in medicine, technology, and many other areas of life provide what appears to be compelling evidence for the idea. Such thinking, coupled with the concept that properly trained intellectuals carefully studying the data would be able to discover truth and then communicate that truth to the less well educated, seems to underlie the various attempts of the so-called Enlightenment project to engineer an ideal society.

A third characteristic of modernity is its **emphasis on and confidence in the individual.** Lundin says, "Whether in the rationalism of Descartes or in the empiricism of Francis Bacon, the philosophical traditions of the early modern period depicted the self as a <u>discoverer</u> of truth. The truth was to be found in the inner regions of the mind and spirit or in the vast phenomena of the natural world."[13]

Modernity's Understanding Of Truth

Modernity understood truth in essentially the same way as had been the case in the premodern world. Both assumed that **there is a real world** and that **truth is that which corresponds to the reality that is there** (sometimes known as the correspondence view of truth[G]). But modernity differed from premodern thought in that modernity was fully confident that humans are capable of discovering the truth and thus understanding the world. The focus on the physical world, together with the assumption that the universe is a closed system (that is, without any supernatural influences) led modernism to suppose that the application of reason to reality would lead to the discovery of **universal and fully coherent principles** (sometimes known as metanarratives[G]). In addition, modernism believed that, given enough time, these accumulated principles would result in a complete understanding of reality. The supposition of modernity was that careful reasoning would lead to knowledge and values in science and the arts — as well as on legal, moral and ethical issues — that every reasonable individual would have to acknowledge as true.

Modernity And The Spirit Of The Age

Modernity has contributed significantly to the zeitgeist[G] (*the spirit of the age*) of the last century, and the characteristics noted above have impacted the entire modern culture. Our culture's devotion to science and technology is apparent in many ways.[14] One of its manifestations is the powerful technological infrastructure that Jacques Ellul (quoted in David Gill's book) calls *Technique*. Gill says,

> Technique is the method of reducing every phenomenon to rational analysis, reducing what is qualitative to quantitative consideration, thinking and working only in terms of measurable results. It is the worship of measurable effectiveness....Dominant in scientific methodology and technology, it rules with equal strength in bureaucracy, advertising, marketing, public relations, psychotherapy and other fields.[15]

It is widely recognized that business decisions are often made on the basis of profit with little consideration of their impact on people; coaches are evaluated on the basis of their won-lost record irrespective of their influence on the character or intellect of their players; success (often even in the church) is assessed largely in terms of external considerations such as money, popularity, measurable performance, physical attractiveness, and so on.

Most people in our society have greater confidence in the assured results of scientific thinking than in tradition, particularly when the traditions include those of the church and Scripture, and much of that skepticism is attributable to the influence of modernity. In fact, the impact of modernity on biblical studies has been particularly dramatic. The same evolution of thinking and method that affected science, philosophy and the zeitgeist[G] in general, also impacted biblical studies. The ideas of Bacon, Descartes, Spinoza, Kant and others were applied to the study of the Bible, and the result was a radical paradigm shift away from that which prevailed during premodern times. According to the new paradigm, ultimate certainty rests only in conclusions based on careful empirical data and irrefutable logic. The final authority for such judgments is the properly educated, rational individual, and his or her opinions take priority over the traditions of uneducated prior generations.

The revelatory claims made by Scripture and affirmed historically by the church seemed to many to be but another example of tradition that could not be accepted at face value. As the scientific method was applied to the study of Scripture it quickly became apparent that there was a significant tension between the two. Biblical claims of miracles and divine intervention into history and the natural process stand quite apart from that which the scientific method is able to examine, and they seemed to contradict the growing consensus that the "cosmos exists as a uniformity of cause and effect in a closed system."[16]

Under the influence of modernity, the basis for authority shifted from Scripture, with its claims to be the special revelation of God, to human reason which carefully applied the scientific method and determined truth by a rigorous rational and empirical examination of the facts. The faith assumptions that had been held by most Christians about the Bible's divine origins were rejected, leaving only the assumption that it was no more authoritative than any other ancient document. The stories of the Bible were taken to be no different from the folklore of other peoples and claims of supernatural activity in history were seen as religious interpretations of events that actually followed the natural laws of cause and effect. Those scholars who saw religious value in the Bible sought to *demythologize* the stories in order to make them more credible to a world committed to the modern perspective. Scholars set out to determine what really happened by the application of scientific method in contrast to the religious interpretation of the events found in the text. This dramatic shift of approach brought about a dichotomy between the *facts* (which had to be determined by modern scholars using the scientific method) and the religious and theological message of the text, still thought to have contemporary religious relevance.

One current example of this approach is the Jesus Seminar, which involves a number of prominent New Testament scholars who are meeting regularly in an effort to determine which words attributed to Jesus in the Gospels he really said and which events reported about him in the New Testament actually occurred. A colleague recently attended one of these meetings as an observer and indicated that these scholars voted unanimously that the resurrection did not actually occur.[17] As Alister McGrath has pointed out, "Where this effort hoped to make mainline Christianity credible to secularists, it ended up making secularism credible to mainline Christians."[18]

The worldview produced by modernity is sometimes called Naturalism, and James Sire summarizes its assumptions:[19]

1. Matter exists and is all there is. The material universe exists and is the sum total of reality. Nothing exists outside of the material world.

2. The universe is a closed system that uniformly operates on the basis of cause and effect.

3. People are highly complex bio-chemical organisms and personality, mental function, artistic creativity—things Christians have always associated with man's spirit or spiritual nature—are solely the result of those bio-chemical processes.

4. Death, the disorganization of the matter that constitutes a person, is the end of personal, individual existence.

5. History is a linear stream of events linked by cause and effect but without an overarching purpose.

6. Ethics and morals are humanly determined. Moral values derive from human experience. Ethics are autonomous and situational and stem only from human need and interest.

The Zeitgeist of Modernity and the Challenge of Christian Thinking

Modern scientific method reflects a very different worldview than that reflected in Scripture, and the implications of this difference in perspective are not lost on McCown:

The nature of divine activity, as seen by the ancient world, was arbitrary, deterministic, and miraculous. God, or the gods, stood outside to foreordain and interfere with the course of events. Modern science and philosophy have no place for miracles and special providences. History is the result of the complex interaction of natural and social forces and the actions and reactions of men. There are neither demons nor angels. God only acts through men. Neither the liberal nor the conservative, neither the historian nor the theologian can afford to neglect this total difference of world view.[20]

Because all scholars, both those committed to the modern and those committed to the premodern paradigms[G], were committed to the same *correspondence* view of truth[G] (the view which says truth is that which corresponds with reality), the tension between the two worldviews is apparent: They differed in what they saw as reality, so they inevitably differed in what they saw as truth. Since our understanding of truth must correspond to what actually exists, the supernatural realm (including angels, demons, and miracles, as the Bible describes them) is either a part of reality — though obviously not susceptible to the analysis of the scientific method — or it is a religious creation that does not correspond to reality, and so does not exist.

Such examples not only set in clear relief the differences between a worldview informed by modernity and one informed by God's special revelation, they also show the importance of faith as a way of knowing truth. It is by faith that we know that God created the world (Gen. 1:1; Heb. 11:3); the methods of modernity cannot demonstrate such truth. It is by faith that we know that a spiritual world exists; the methods of modernity cannot discover such reality. It is by faith that we know God is bringing history to the conclusion that he sovereignly desires; modernity and scientific method cannot establish the truth or falsity of such claims. It is by faith that we know that personal existence does not end with the death of the body; such questions are beyond the scope of the methods promoted by modernity. It is by faith that we know that people are made for a right relationship with God and how that right relationship comes about; modernity is not able to provide answers to such essential questions about human existence. Many of the truth claims of the Bible cannot be validated by the methods of modernity and they must be accepted by faith if they are to be affirmed as true. Thus the worldview of modernity and a biblically informed one differ not only in what they understand to be true, but also in their epistemology[G] (how we know truth); a biblically informed worldview recognizes the importance of faith in knowing truth (that is, the epistemological significance of faith).

As Shapiro notes, the scientific method "neither denies nor excludes the possibility of the supernatural; it <u>ignores</u> it. Since a supernatural Creator by definition falls outside the realm accessible to scientific method, science per se neither affirms nor denies the existence of God."[21] While there is no theoretical denial of the supernatural in modernity, there is a pragmatic denial that trivializes such belief. By arguing that the only things that can be known with certainty are things that are empirically proved or those things that are logically irrefutable, the supernatural is marginalized and excluded from those matters that can be confidently affirmed. Or to put it differently, while science *says* it has no opinion on the existence of God, it *acts* as if it were certain that God does not exist.

Modernity's emphasis on the individual gives rise to what Thomas Oden calls "autonomous individualism"[22] in which man becomes the highest value and the ultimate authority for truth and morality. Oden says, "Narcissism is the key mark of modernity. Myself becomes the central project of moral interest; self-enjoyment and self-development become the central goals."[23] This radical individualism[G] contributes to the lack of community found throughout modern society;[24] it contributes to the selfishness that pervades society as individual fulfillment and desire override loyalty to relationships and community responsibility. The hyper-individualism of modernity feeds the pervasive materialism of modern culture as people scramble to get all the newest clothes and gadgets that effective marketing convinces them they deserve. The influence of modernity in the church is often seen in those who have little loyalty to a local church and who continue to go only so long as they are entertained and their "needs are met."[25]

B. F. Skinner sought to apply scientific method rigorously to the study of human behavior. Since he believed that human beings are simply bio-chemical organisms and since for everything that happens there is a natural cause, Skinner argued for a rigid psychological determinism that concluded that all human choices are determined by genetic and environmental factors. Thus what appear to us to be *choices* are in fact just the responses of an organism to its environment. The implications of this view are that people have neither freedom nor dignity, and they thus have no responsibility for their behavior. These ideas, driven by the assumptions of modernity, express themselves in society in many different ways in education, in the criminal justice system, and they seem to underlie the idea that everyone is a victim with no responsibility for his or her actions. Such ideas clearly present a challenge for the believer who wants to understand the reality of what it means to be a human being, and because the ideas are so pervasive it is difficult to avoid their influence.

Modernity rejected biblical revelation (which it saw as merely religious tradition) as the basis for morality, arguing instead that reason and careful study could produce moral values that are so compelling as to be recognized as valid by virtually everyone in society. What modernity anticipated, however, failed to materialize, and what resulted was a moral relativism[G]. Divorced from any absolute basis for morality, such as divine revelation provides, reason was unable to override the worldviews and desires of each individual (scholars included) to produce the consensus that was hoped for as to what was acceptable moral behavior and what a good society should be like.

The failures of modernity in this regard are set in clear relief by the possibilities that modern technology has created. Technology has produced the tools to destroy civilization, and modern history attests to the fact that the moral values that have come out of modernity have not always been able to direct that technology into channels that contribute to the progress of civilization. Medical technology offers the potential for manipulating humans in ways never imagined possible even decades ago and again the moral and ethical responses regularly lag far behind the technology.[26] Modernity challenges the believer in that it challenges biblical faith as the final authority in matters of morality, thereby eliminating an absolute basis for such values. At the same time modernity calls into question many of the moral givens of both Scripture and the church. While the church needs to continue to think carefully and critically about its values and make adjustments where that is needed, it must not be deceived into forsaking the one authoritative basis that it has for moral decision making, God's revealed truth. The influence of modernity is both powerful and pervasive, and there are many signs that the church is affected by modernity's approach to morals. The changing moral standards practiced by many in the church, and the widespread tendency of many in the church to substitute personal preference and intuition for the authoritative voice of Scripture in determining morality, affirms the influence of modernity among God's people.

The naturalistic worldview of modernity which has dominated much thinking in the modern Western world is clearly incompatible with the Christian faith at many points, and a biblically informed worldview will part company with much modern thinking over a number of issues. Certainly the evangelical church has not bought into those assumptions of modernity that overtly contradict the essentials of the faith. At the same time the effects of modernity are quite pervasive and its influence very likely has impacted the worldview of even the most careful believer.

Questions For Further Consideration:

1. Can you think of areas of your life where you feel pressured by modernity's demand for measurable results?

2. Are there times where the values of modernity make it difficult to maintain the priorities that as a Christian you feel are essential?

3. Can you think of instances where reason and evidence create tension with conclusions based on your faith? How do you resolve the tension?

4. Imagine that you have been examined by a competent physician who tells you that you have a serious disease. You feel great and cannot believe that the doctor is right. What would it take to convince you that the doctor's scientific evidence is more reliable than the way you feel?

5. Your pastor points you to a passage that seems to clearly teach something different than what you have always assumed was true and that several professors over the years have affirmed as well. What would it take to convince you that something clearly taught in Scripture is more reliable than the evidence you are aware of which is also consistent with the way you feel?

6. A friend tells you she has been informed by her doctor that she has a serious illness and tells you that she and her church have prayed about this and she is convinced that she is completely

healed. How would you respond? What would you conclude about the *truth* in this situation?

Notes

[1]Thomas Oden, *Agenda for Theology After Modernity...What?* (Grand Rapids, Michigan: Zondervan, 1990), p. 44.

[2]Arthur Shapiro, "God and Science, *The Pennsylvania Gazette* (October, 1987), 47.

[3]*Ibid.*

[4]Some have called this approach the "God of the gaps" idea since God is brought in to fill in the gaps of our understanding. Charles Hummel (*The Galileo Connection* [Downers Grove, Illinois], pp. 179-97) has argued for a more integrated view of reality in which God's sovereign oversight is recognized as much in those phenomena we can account for on the basis of natural laws of cause and effect as in the apparently miraculous that we cannot explain on that basis. Such a view seems to give God the place he occupies in the biblical perspective.

[5]Walsh and Middleton, *The Transforming Vision* (Downers Grove, Illinois: InterVarsity Press, 1984), p. 124.

[6]Lundin, *Culture of Interpretation*, pp. 42-47.

[7]Andrew Walker, *Enemy Territory* (Grand Rapids, Michigan: Zondervan, 1987), pp. 79-80.

[8]According to Lundin (*Ibid.*, pp. 246-47), Descartes and other rationalist philosophers actually "were seeking to strengthen belief rather than to undermine faith, but by claiming that reason builds a stronger foundation for faith than the one provided by church, tradition, and the Scriptures, the early modern philosophers helped pave the way for postmodern disbelief."

[9]Harvey, *Condition of Postmodernity*, p. 13.

[10]*Ibid.*, p. 12.

[11]Shapiro, "God And Science," p. 50.

[12]Again the great advances made in medicine, technology, and many other areas of life often make this idea difficult to resist.

[13]Lundin, *Culture of Interpretation*, p. 53.

[14]See Walsh and Middleton, *Transforming Vision*, pp. 131-140.

[15]Gill, *Opening of the Christian Mind*, p. 41.

[16]James Sire, *The Universe Next Door* (Downers Grove, Illinois: InterVarsity Press, 1976), p. 62. Note also Shapiro's statement ("God and Science," p. 51) that "One is able to do science at all only if one accepts certain intrinsically unprovable postulates about the universe." One of those postulates is "that the universe is lawful; and that its laws are and always have been the same everywhere."

[17]For an evangelical response to such "scholarship" dominated by the assumptions of modernity, see J. P. Moreland and Mike Wilkins, eds., *Jesus Under Fire* (Zondervan, 1995).

[18]Alister McGrath, "Why Evangelicalism is the Future of Protestantism," *Christianity Today* (June 19, 1995), p. 20.

[19]The summary is taken from Sire, *The Universe Next Door*, pp. 58-75.

[20]C. C. McCown, "The Current Plight of Biblical Scholarship," *Journal of Biblical Literature* (1956), 18.

[21]Shapiro, "Creation and Science," p. 51.

[22]Thomas Oden, "On Not Whoring After the Spirit of the Age," in *No Gods But God*, ed. by Guinness and Seel, p. 193.

[23]Oden, *After Modernity*, p. 79.

[24]See Gill's comments (*Opening of the Christian Mind*, pp. 96-97).

[25]James Berkley ("The Marketing of a Boomer Church," *Christianity Today* [February 11, 1991], p. 34) says, "A notable baby boomer characteristic is a lack of institutional loyalty." He quotes Leith Anderson, the pastor of a church that targets its entire program to this group, "The loyalty of a baby boomer must be won on a weekly basis. If you've gained the loyalty of people born in the first quarter of this century, generally they'll stick with you. But the boomers, raised on consumerism, will switch brands if they find a better deal."

[26]For a useful discussion, see Kenneth Schemmer, *Tinkering With People* (Victor Books, 1992).

CHAPTER 4

Postmodernism And The Challenge To Christian Thinking

Modernity, which has long been the major contributor to the prevailing zeitgeist of Western culture, has begun to give way to more recent ideas, all of them often referred to by the general term *postmodernism.*

It is clear that modernity and the Enlightenment project have not delivered on their promises. While technology has produced immense benefits for people, and increased knowledge continues to give humans mastery over various parts of their environment, it has become apparent that the reductionism^G of modernity was defective. The claim that only that which is empirically and/or rationally justified can be confidently affirmed as true led to a reductionism that excluded many important parts of life from serious consideration in academic discussion. The relational and aesthetic dimensions of life were generally neglected, as were the spiritual and the moral. The current state of affairs in the west is compelling evidence that the formulas of modernity that were supposed to lead to peace, prosperity and happiness throughout the world were missing some crucial elements.

The French Revolution, the Communist experiment, Nazi Germany, the nuclear age, the environmental crisis, and political and economic problems around the world have made it increasingly clear that modernity is incapable of dealing with many issues essential to civilized life. At the level of the ordinary individual, the lack of a spiritual element in modernity may well account for the increased use of harmful illicit drugs, the growing crime rate, and a general sense of malaise.[1] Increased knowledge has not brought us closer to the kinds of comprehensive explanations and solutions modernity was seeking. Rather, it has further demonstrated how limited our understanding is. Modernity has brought a complexity to life that appears to have created more problems than it has solved.

Oden says,

> Modern history is turning out to be embarrassing precisely on the basis of its own optimistic axioms. Not some theory of history but actual modern history is what is killing the ideology of modernity. I need mention only Auschwitz, Mylai, Solzhenitsyn's Gulag Archipelago, Hustler magazine, the assault statistics in public schools, the juvenile suicide rate, or cocaine babies. All these point to the depth of failure of modern consciousness. While modernity continues blandly to teach us that we are moving ever upward and onward, the actual history of late modernity is increasingly brutal, barbarian, and malignant.[2]

There is widespread empirical evidence that modernity has failed, and postmodern responses to modernity are quite varied. They range from isolated reactions to specific claims or abuses of modernity to more broad and philosophically based critiques that sometimes involve radical and militant dimensions. When postmodernism is defined simply as that which follows modernity,[3] the movement often offers helpful insight into the exaggerations and overly optimistic claims and goals of modernity; other forms of postmodernism include philosophical currents that are far more problematic.

Critics Of Modernity

In addition to the empirical evidence that points to modernity's failure to deliver on its claims, postmodern thinking has been influenced significantly by the thinking of philosophers like Immanuel Kant. As Poythress points out, Kant argued that "Whatever we observed empirically, we observed in terms of categories presupposed by the human mind...human experience necessarily conformed to preestablished categories of the mind."[4] Thus, Kant's ideas challenged claims about the mind's ability to accurately understand reality. Kant argued "that the self does not so much <u>discover</u> preexisting order in the world as it <u>projects</u>

order creatively upon the world."[5] The greater implications of Kant's idea are expressed by Rorty when he says, "About two hundred years ago, the idea that truth was made rather than found began to take hold of the imagination in Europe."[6] This radical shift in epistemology[G] (how we know truth) is a fundamental break from the assumptions of modernity and has contributed significantly to the postmodern negative reaction to modernity.

Postmodern thought also draws deeply from the work of Friedrich Nietzsche who, like Kant, questioned man's ability to perceive truth in a highly complex and chaotic world. He argued that all attempts to determine meaning are doomed to failure and that truth is radically relative. As Lundin points out,

> For Nietzsche and his ideological descendants, all knowledge is a matter of perspective; that is, it is a matter of interpretation and all interpretations are lies. It would be impossible for matters to be otherwise, because Nietzsche would argue that the only relationship of language to reality,...is that which has been established by acts of violence and power through the agencies of habit and convention."[7]

Ideas regularly encountered in postmodernism are Nietzsche's emphasis on the chaos of life, and his idea that *truth is defined by some group within society*[8] and then imposed on the rest of the community.[9] Related to these ideas is the recognition that human perception and observation is a matter of perspective and is colored by the observer's context. People see what they are looking for; they see what the paradigms in which they have been trained cause them to expect.[10]

Lundin suggests that this "Perspectivism[G]" is a fundamental characteristic of postmodernism. He defines Perspectivism as "the theory that knowledge of a subject is inevitably partial and limited by the individual perspective from which it is viewed."[11] Lundin also notes the comments of Robert Solomon: "This peculiar view, which sometimes parades under the title 'epistemological nihilism,' is in fact a form of relativism, or what Nietzsche calls his 'perspectivism' — the view that there are only truths for a certain sort of creature or a certain society, there is no truth as such."[12] Such an understanding does much to support a relativistic pluralism[G], in which each person's perception differs because his understanding is determined by his social contexts; therefore, no ultimate judgments can be made about the legitimacy of each perspective. Richard Rorty talks about that distinctly postmodern intellectual "attitude [which is] interested not so much in what is out there in the world, or in what happened in history, as in what we can get out of nature and history for our own uses."[13] This attitude leads to what Lundin calls a *therapeutic culture*, about which he says,

> [It is] one in which questions of ultimate concern—about the nature of good, the meaning of truth, and the existence of God—are taken to be unanswerable and hence in some fundamental sense insignificant. A therapeutic culture focuses upon the management of experience and environment in the interest of [a] 'manipulatable sense of well-being.'[14]

Postmodernism's View Of Language

Nietzsche also argued that language consists only of metaphors[G] and has no objective connection with reality. He thus denied that language can communicate truth about reality. He did, though, see language as an important means by which the *truth* defined by a certain community imposes that understanding on others. As Lundin notes, "Since all uses of language involve deception, Nietzsche claims, one can do nothing more than seek to dissemble with power and effectiveness. According to Nietzsche, one lies for the purpose of satisfying one's desires or deepest needs."[15] Obviously Nietzsche ignores the many accurate uses of language that function satisfactorily in our everyday lives.[16] Clearly Nietzsche's idea denies the validity of scriptural truth expressed as it is in human language.

This idea leads to another important feature of postmodernism. Since language is seen as incapable of communicating truth with perfect accuracy, and since *truth* is defined by various social and political groups, it becomes important to identify the power structures that have created *truth*, and then through language, used that truth to oppress and permanently marginalize those outside the structure. The effective use of language offers to those oppressed groups (postmodern groups like women, ethnic minorities, and homosexuals) the prospect for liberation, and a voice that they hope will break the bonds of oppression and lead them to liberation and power. An important purpose of education that follows from this view is to help students identify the sources of oppression and to free themselves and their culture from that oppression.[17] As Lundin[18] notes, these postmodern advocacy groups often feel little need to prove their claims rationally concerning what is true. Since it is not possible to discover truth in the Enlightenment sense, and since language could not communicate it anyway, such groups sometimes show little interest in academic rigor and in providing supporting evidence for their claims. Instead, they simply use language and politics to further their agenda.

The view of language espoused by postmodernism gives rise to another sort of skepticism as well. The idea that the author of a piece of literature could communicate a message that a reader could then understand seems absurd to those advocating the postmodern understanding of truth and language. Thus, the meaning of a piece of literature is the meaning each reader creates from his or her reading of the piece. A reader of Shakespeare's *Hamlet* who is also a serial murderer (to take an extreme but possible example) may interpret the play as a defense of Claudius who killed his brother and king. The reader might then go on to see the play as a diatribe against young Hamlet who seems to think it important to identify his father's murderer and see that he is punished. The fact that the text of the play as we have it, together with the historical and sociological background of its composition, must be violently distorted to support this reading is deemed irrelevant by this sort of postmodernism. There is no objectively determined meaning, and in postmodern thought a piece of literature can mean anything a reader decides it means, and it can have as many meanings as an interpreter wants to assign to it. To many postmodernists every meaning is equally valid and equally *true*. Further examples of this kind of thinking are seen in the books and movies that present a revisionist history of a certain event or historical era in order to further a certain political agenda.

We see then that much of postmodern thought involves the rejection of several fundamental presuppositions of modernity. The seeds planted by Kant and Nietzsche resulted in a radically different epistemology than is found in modernism. Modernism assumed that there is a real world and that careful study of that world results in the discovery of truth that corresponds to reality. Kant's epistemology cast doubt on the ability of the human mind to discover truth and instead argued that the human mind creates truth internally and organizes reality according to the categories it creates. Nietzsche cast further doubt on the possibility that humans could understand the chaos of reality and denied that language can communicate any truth about reality. He argued that *truth* is created by a community that then uses its power to impose its own ideas on others.

While modernity sought overarching theories that would collect diverse bits of data and tie them together in a coherent whole, postmodern thinking denies the possibility of finding such a unifying explanation and is characterized by the metaphor[G] of collage and disconnectedness. Harvey says that postmodernism is marked by "its total acceptance of the ephemerality, fragmentation, discontinuity and the chaotic."[19] And, he notes, "it does not try to transcend it, counteract it, or even try to define the 'eternal and immutable' elements that might lie within it. Postmodernism swims, even wallows, in the fragmentary and the chaotic currents of change as if that is all there is."[20] The elements in the collage are taken apart (deconstructed) and moved into constantly changing arrangements. New elements are introduced from quite unexpected sources, never in order to achieve a closer correspondence with reality, but rather to contribute to a variety of individual and group agendas.

Postmodernism And Education

In such a postmodern culture the goals and methods of education are quite different from what they had been under the Enlightenment model. As was noted above, particular attention is given to analysis of the political agendas that underlie every truth claim, and significant effort is directed toward identifying the sources and methods of the oppression that has impacted society in general and the marginalized in particular.

The spirit of Enlightenment education is characterized by what Richard Hofstadter and Walter Metzger have called "norms of neutrality and competence."[21] The American Association of University Professors' statement on academic freedom states that conclusions set forth in the classroom must reflect proper scholarly method ("they must be the pursuits of competent and patient and sincere inquiry"). In addition divergent opinions should be set forth fairly. The scholar should remember "that his business is not to provide his students with ready-made conclusions but to train them to think for themselves, and to provide them with access to those materials which they need if they are to think intelligently."[22]

Higher education has generally recognized that people at early stages of cognitive development gain their understanding of what is true from what authority figures (parents, teachers, and certain others) tell them is true. They then move to a different method of knowing in which they realize that their own minds are significant resources. They begin to question many of the positions imposed on them by authorities and to make independent judgments about what is true. At this point their understanding of what is true generally contains a strong subjective and intuitive component. An important task of higher education has been to help students understand that many opinions about what is true exist in the world and that all of them are not necessarily equal. As educators have made students aware of the diversity of views about what is true that come from those who claim to know, they have also sought to train students in the methods of their disciplines, methods that attempt to eliminate bias and allow a somewhat objective assessment of reality. One of the highest priorities of Enlightenment education has been teaching students to think critically[23] and carefully in order to equip them to evaluate competing truth claims. This approach to education presupposes that there is a real world to which we have access through reason and our senses. It presupposes that human beings carefully using those faculties can at least approach and approximate the reality that exists and to which truth must correspond.

In the postmodern model, truth is unattainable. It is contextually dependent; it is determined by an interpretive community, and it reflects a political agenda. Under such an understanding disciplines like German or biology or math can still be pursued in the traditional way as long as we understand that the rules we are learning and applying are pragmatic,[24] limited, and are true only because the community of scholars that make up the discipline have agreed as to what constitutes *truth* in that discipline.

Since, according to postmodern thinking, truth is unknowable and ideas cannot be separated from a political agenda, the focus of education is often transformed by postmodern thought. Cheney says,

> For decades educators have affirmed the idea that higher education should be about seeking evidence, evaluating it critically, weighing conflicting opinions — about trying to tell what is true. But this aim is frequently derided today. An increasingly influential view is that there is no truth to tell: What we think of as truth is merely a cultural construct, serving to empower some and oppress others. Since power and politics are part of every quest for knowledge...professors are perfectly justified in using the classroom to advance political agendas.[25]

The change in values described by Cheney is made clear by Betty Jean Craige. She reflects on the words of University of Chicago President William Rainey Harper in 1900: "A professor abuses his privilege who takes advantage of a classroom exercise to propagate the partisan view of one or another of the political parties."

> Craige comments that such statements represent an older "dualist" view that assumes that truth can be pursued apart from politics. Now, however, there has been a "paradigm shift from dualism to holism," and a younger generation of professors, for whom the 1960's were a formative era, holds that there is no truth apart from politics, no way to separate truth from ideology. Since education, like all intellectual activity, is always in the service of politics of some sort, faculty members who want to use the classroom to produce "citizens eager to reform social structures" are justified in doing so.[26]

Theoretically, under Enlightenment values any position for which there is evidential and logical support should be welcome in the University. While the postmodern approach would seem to welcome every idea irrespective of whether or not there is evidence to support the idea, in practice the use of language to further one's political agenda, apart from concerns about truth, seems to control the application. The most radical results of the shift from Enlightenment values to postmodern ones are seen in those who make no attempt to preserve balance of fairness and who rewrite history or the facts to support their own agendas.

MacIntyre argues that "'post-Enlightenment relativism^G and perspectivism'^G is the 'negative counterpart of the Enlightenment, its inverted mirror image.' The power of relativism in contemporary intellectual life derives from its 'inversion of certain central Enlightenment positions concerning truth and rationality.'"[27] Many postmodern critiques of modernity deny that humans can in any objective sense determine truth; they deny that there are any overarching theories that tie knowledge together in a coherent way; and they deny that language has the capability to accurately communicate truth. The moral relativity that modernity fostered by divorcing morality from divine revelation continues in postmodernism though it is now connected with postmodernism's denial that truth can be discovered; like any other *truth* in postmodernism, morality is simply a construct of the culture or some special interest group. Modernity's elevation of the individual to an almost godlike status continues in postmodernism though now it is focused differently; the ability of the individual to determine truth rationally and creatively is transformed so that personal preference and the satisfaction of personal desire become the ultimate good.

The Zeitgeist of Postmodernism and the Challenge of Christian Thinking

Some of the major components that postmodernism has contributed to the zeitgeist are clear. In some ways, though, it is more difficult to assess the impact of this movement on the evangelical community than it is to see how modernity has impacted it. This difficulty is the case because postmodernism's relative newness provides less chance for hindsight. In addition, postmodernism continues to evolve and express itself in far more varied ways than modernity.

Postmodernism's critique of modernity's exaggerated claims also offers much from which evangelicals can benefit. Modernity's idea that human beings through the application of reason can fully understand reality and exercise mastery over their environment is incompatible with the biblical doctrines of man's finiteness (that is, his natural limitations) and fallenness, and it seems to be at variance with the biblical doctrine of God's sovereignty as well. Such thinking reflects a refusal to acknowledge that human beings are creatures rather than the Creator. Modernity has perhaps turned our attention away from realities about our creatureliness and the limits of our understanding of life, the world, and the activity of God. Postmodernism offers us a reminder of our own limits and the complexities of reality that should encourage a greater caution in dogmatically proclaiming our comprehensive understanding of truth. Postmodern critiques should motivate us to include in our thinking and practice a place for ambiguity and for what Job and Ecclesiastes teach about human inability to understand and control many aspects of reality.

A growing awareness of the complexities of reality and of our own finiteness should bring us to a deeper appreciation for multidimensional approaches, each of which captures some aspect of the truth that corresponds to reality. As Sire points out, questions about such basic realities as, "What is a human being?" "are addressed by literature, linguistics, history, philosophy, physics, chemistry, biology, physiology, psychology, sociology, theology and so forth. Each provides a glimpse."[28] This multidimensional approach to knowledge is a way of combining the strengths of both modernity and postmodernism in that it seeks a reality independent of human thought, but it also recognizes that the limits of human perspective force us to see a thing from as many different vantage points as possible. It is only when all the glimpses are combined that anything approaching a comprehensive understanding can be attained. Also, different individuals and different cultural perspectives can provide invaluable insights.

This approach is perhaps reflected in Scripture in the various images used to communicate truth about the reality of salvation. Salvation is described using a number of metaphors such as redemption, justification, regeneration, propitiation, adoption, and so on, each of which captures important truth without, it would seem, necessarily giving us exhaustive knowledge about the reality of a right relationship with God. Such awareness should help to deliver us from the mistake of Job's friends in failing to distinguish between true truth about God and his work on the one hand, and comprehensive truth about those matters on the other.

Postmodernism's emphasis on the way communities, including the church, have used language and ideas as a mechanism for manipulation and control should cause the church to examine its own history and present practice more carefully in order to minimize such abuse and make the evangelical community a place where diverse individuals and groups are welcomed as fully participating members. The church's need for sensitivity and an increased openness to the pain of the marginalized should result from our awareness of the legitimacy of postmodernism's critique.[29]

Modernism eliminated the spiritual from serious discussion by its demand for rational and empirical proof, and postmodernism recognizes the weakness of limiting one's focus to those matters that can be proved in the laboratory or proved logically. At the same time the discussions of the spiritual pursued by many followers of postmodernism often involve New Age thinking and mysticism of various kinds, and the radical relativism of postmodernism puts every perspective on equal footing. A friend recently told me about a television program he saw that presents the postmodern perspective. The show involved a doctor working in a small town in the West during the last century. As the doctor worked at trying to bring medical science to a community skeptical of such things, the doctor became ill and was unable to diagnose the illness and find a cure. The doctor finally took the advice of the medicine man which resulted in the needed cure. Similar stories reflecting the postmodern criticism of the thinking of modernity are often encountered in movies and modern literature.

The popularity of books on near death experiences (e.g., Betty Eadie's book, *Embraced by the Light*) also reflects the greater openness to such ideas that exists in a postmodern culture. Many of these books are based on the author's own experience and contain many non-biblical ideas.[30] Such books and the media coverage that they generate often have a powerful effect on the worldviews of many people. The discussions deal with a subject that has profound emotional appeal for those struggling with the loss of a loved one, and they do so in a way that gives great comfort to people by telling them what they want to hear. These experiences rarely seem to deal with issues such as sin, judgment or Hell.

Postmodernism's emphasis on the sociology of knowledge should make us more aware of our lack of objectivity and cause us to carefully examine our worldview and the influences that have contributed to it. Such awareness should lead to a greater openness to other perspectives and to an understanding of the insight that those perspectives can bring to our understanding. This process is also crucial in ferreting out the non-Christian assumptions that we all hold. Such an understanding is essential in interpreting Scripture. As Lundin points out,

> We are creatures who have received hosts of assumptions about ourselves and about the nature of things; we are connected with vast communities, past and present, whether or not we will these connections or are even aware of them.

> Prejudices, then, serve as the necessary foundation for all understanding. The goal of all thinking, and reading, should not be to cast these assumptions aside....Rather, the goal of thinking and reading is to test, clarify, modify, and expand our assumptions in order to bring them more in line with the truth of things.

> According to Gadamer, human understanding is most fruitfully conceived of as a form of dialogue in which the horizon of our prejudices is fused with that of the other's as we both gaze upon the object of truth in question...one looks with another upon the object and enters into dialogue in search of understanding.[31]

The awareness of the effect of biases and assumptions on interpretation should cause us to recognize our need for others in the interpretive process. It should motivate us to seek out the insights of saints throughout history as well those whose traditions differ from us, and it should do this in order to enter into a dialogue that hopefully will bring us to a more accurate understanding of the truth contained in both general and special revelation and to a better understanding of how to appropriately apply this truth to life.

Postmodernism's emphasis on the ambiguity of language and the difficulties in interpreting language should be taken seriously by evangelicals as well. Often our **interpretations** are glibly presented as if they were as certain as the **data of Scripture**, and people are misled into supposing that the dimensions of our metanarratives[G] are greater than they actually are. People are deceived by our failure to make clear that there is ambiguity in many of the passages that we confidently proclaim and that our interpretations are sometimes less than certain. While many evangelicals view these developments with concern, some evangelical scholars are beginning to emphasize both the necessity and the benefits of a plurality of interpretations,[32] while at the same time rejecting the interpretive skepticism and relativism of postmodernism.

Problematic Influences Of Postmodernism

The influences of postmodernism are not wholly beneficial. While postmodernism's legitimate criticisms of the abuses and exaggerated claims of modernity serve as useful reminders for evangelicals who have allowed the zeitgeist of modernity to influence their thought and practice inappropriately, postmodernism presents its own significant dangers to the Christian community. In particular, those forms of the movement that have their roots in the philosophy of Kant and Nietzsche appear to be no less reductionistic than was modernity. In part because these forms of postmodernism are current in academic circles, they have the potential for broadly impacting the culture as drastically as was the case with modernity.

While modernity concluded that rational human beings can discover ultimate truth, postmodernism concludes that they cannot do so and that "all of the identities dealt with cognitively and practically in the world around us are products of our mind."[33] While modernity claimed the ability to uncover comprehensive and universally applicable metanarratives, postmodernism argues that no overarching theories are possible. Modernity shared with the premodern world the assumption that accurate human communication is possible, while postmodernism under the influence of Neitzsche and Derrida argue that human language cannot accurately communicate truth and that language is only the servant of politics. Clearly a number of the assumptions of postmodernism have profound implications for worldview, and a Christian must think very carefully about whether those assumptions are compatible with a biblically informed worldview.

A worldview that recognizes significant limits on the ability of human beings to perceive truth or that questions the possibility of people ever arriving at an understanding of ultimate truth on their own may or may not be correct in its details, but it is not fundamentally incompatible with Christian orthodoxy. A worldview that reduces *all* human knowledge to constructions of the mind and to politics seems to fly in the face of fundamental claims of special revelation. If these biblical claims are correct, then there is the possibility of at least some metanarratives[G] (again, known by faith). In view of the history of human thought and the model of humanness presupposed by the Old Testament wisdom literature and much of the rest of Scripture, it seems clear that human interaction with general revelation through reason and empirical means can produce significant understanding and knowledge. While the correspondence theory of truth[G] may not be the final answer to the question, "What is truth?"[34] the reductionism[G] of postmodernism is also a defect when it excludes entirely any possibility of a correct understanding of reality.

Extreme forms of postmodern epistemology lead to a radical pessimism and relativism[G] as each person or group perceives things in a way compatible with their agenda with no way to judge objectively whether one opinion or *truth* is more valid than another. Such a worldview is clearly incompatible with the claims of biblical religion. Faith allows us to recognize certain values as correct because they come into human history as God's revealed word. Special revelation affirms that there are some things that are absolutely and ultimately true and that we can know some of them because God has revealed them to his people. Certainly the church has often failed to distinguish between biblical givens and cultural values, and the result has been a failure to value experiences and opinions that diverge from those of the dominant culture. While postmodernism is extremely helpful in calling us to examine our presuppositions and biases and in calling us to listen to other voices both within and without the community, the solution is not found in a radical postmodern epistemology that denies that there is any objective basis for passing judgment on competing truth claims. The church needs to hear the postmodern call that affirms and encourages the pursuit of the agendas of those at the margins of the dominant culture. At the same time, such an approach also has the potential for further dividing the church rather than contributing to the unity that is the biblical ideal. The church must listen to minority voices and be open to their critiques and cries; the church must be willing to respond and change when change is needed. At the same time, minorities must be equally committed to listening to the corrective voice of Scripture as the entire church moves toward the unity that the Spirit produces and that God desires.

Finally, the radical postmodern skepticism about the possibility of human communication has far reaching implications for the church; God did, after all, choose to communicate his truth through human language. If we accept the postmodern voices, then any possible benefits provided through God's special revelation in Scripture are negated by the impossibility of accurately interpreting that message, and the meaning of the message becomes whatever the interpreter claims it to be. Postmodern voices are correct in emphasizing the complexities of communication, and they stand as an important warning against an overly simplistic hermeneutic and a failure to understand the ambiguities and uncertainties often inherent in interpretation. Furthermore, these critiques have contributed to important refinements in hermeneutical method as modern evangelical scholars emphasize the need for appropriate consideration of the original author's intention, the text, and the reader's perspective in interpretation. The importance of attempting to reconstruct the original author's historical and cultural context is recognized as well. Evangelicals have learned important principles and techniques from their dialogues with postmodern critics.[35]

At the same time, evangelicals must not be deceived by the skepticism of postmodern thought about interpretation and language. As Lundin points out, "contemporary theories of literature, language, and culture appear to be so intrigued by the deceptive possibilities of language that they are always in danger of forgetting its power to reveal truth."[36] We must, in other words, do two things at once: constantly keep in mind the extreme difficulties inherent in human communication, while also, despite the difficulties, continue to do our best at using language.

While at first glance this may seem contradictory or demoralizing, a moment's reflection will reveal any number of things we do every day under such difficult circumstances — as parents rearing children in a difficult world, for example. We must strive for perfection while simultaneously not expecting to achieve it.

At all times, evangelicals must understand the philosophical underpinnings of much that is called postmodernism and the dangers such thinking poses for the believing community. The radical skepticism about the possibility of understanding truth; the insistence that truth is always made rather than discovered; the radical skepticism about the ability of language to accurately communicate truth; the reduction of all understanding to political terms; all are highly problematic in the light of biblical faith. Evangelicals in a postmodern world must not lose sight of the implications of such biblical doctrines as creation and God's sovereignty, God's special revelation of himself in human culture and through human language, people's creation in the image of God, human finiteness and depravity, the nature of faith as a valid means of knowing truth and a host of other doctrines that impact our understanding of truth and reality. We must carefully and critically evaluate the implications of postmodernism's claims and then thoughtfully integrate those we have accepted into our thinking and practice. However, many of its claims must be rejected or significantly modified as we seek to know the truth and apply it to life.

Questions For Further Consideration:

1. Where do you see evidence around you of the pluralism that characterizes postmodernism? Where do you see examples of moral relativism, cultural relativism, or religious relativism? Does such thinking ever impact the church?

2. Describe a social or work situation in which you had to interact and share ideas with people of different worldviews. How were their assumptions about life different from yours? How did you react to the situation? Do you think the different perspectives reflected in the situation were legitimate?

3. What one scene from television, movies or literature comes to your mind as typifying pluralism in society? What problems of pluralism and postmodernity were revealed? What strengths?

4. Does the relativism promoted by postmodernism tend to undermine genuine biblical faith? Why or why not?

5. In what ways has the worldview of modernity failed you in your life? Are there aspects of postmodernism that seem to work better for you? What aspects of postmodernism seem problematic to you?

6. How justified is a professor in promoting his or her views in a class? Do you think the professor should be required to present a number of views fairly and be open to views with which he disagrees? What would be your reaction to a professor who promoted political or religious views with which you agreed? How would you react in a case where the professor's view opposed yours and your grade suffered as a result?

Notes

[1] As we noted in the previous chapter, the elimination of God from discussions of morality did not lead to consensus, rather it led to a moral relativism where every person does what is right in his own eyes. Note also the comments of Paul in Romans 1:28-32 as he discussed what happens morally when people refuse to acknowledge God.

[2] Oden, *After Modernity*, p. 51.

[3] Diogenes Allen, "The End of the Modern World," *Christian Scholar's Review* 22 (1993), 340. Allen defines Postmodernity as "after the modern world."

[4] Poythress, *Science and Hermeneutics*, p. 28. See also Lundin, *Culture of Interpretation*, pp. 49-52.

[5] Lundin, p. 50.

[6] Richard Rorty, *Contingency, Irony, and Solidarity*, p. 3. Cited by Lundin, *Culture of Interpretation*, p. 41.

[7] Lundin, p. 38.

[8] It could be a government or an academic community or any

other kind of special interest group.

[9]This could be done by the power of effective argument or through political means or any other kind of manipulation that was effective.

[10]On this see Thomas Kuhn, *The Structure of Scientific Revolutions*, 2nd ed. (Chicago: University of Chicago Press, 1970); and Peter Berger and Thomas Luckmann, *The Social Construction of Reality* (New York: Doubleday, 1966).

[11]Lundin, *Cultures of Interpretation*, p. 32, n. 1, quoting the Oxford Dictionary Supplement.

[12]*Ibid.*, citing Robert Solomon, *Continental Philosophy Since 1750: The Rise and Fall of the Self* (Oxford: Oxford University Press, 1988), p. 116.

[13]Lundin, p. 35, quoting Richard Rorty, *Philosophy and the Mirror of Nature* (Princeton: Princeton University Press, 1979), p. 325.

[14]Lundin, pp. 5-6. The term "manipulatable sense of well-being" is taken from Philip Rieff, *The Triumph of the Therapeutic: Uses of Faith After Freud* (New York: Harper & Row, 1966), p. 13.

[15]Lundin, p. 38.

[16]This will be discussed in more detail in chapter 6.

[17]Despite the fact that advocates of this view have given up on the possibility that anything other than a socially determined and therefore relative truth can be found, they seem quite confident that they can identify sources of oppression for everyone.

[18]Lundin, *Culture of Interpretation*, pp. 21-26.

[19]*Harvey*, p. 44.

[20]*Ibid.*

[21]Richard Hofstadter and Walter Metzger, *The Development of Academic Freedom in the United States* (New York: Columbia University Press, 1955), p. 410, cited by Lynne Cheney, Chairman, "Telling the Truth: A Report on the State of the Humanities in Higher Education," 1992, p. 29.

[22]Louis Joughin, ed. "The 1915 Declaration of Principles," *Academic Freedom and Tenure: A Handbook of the American Association of University Professors*, p. 169, cited by Cheney, p. 30.

[23]As Baird and Soden have pointed out critical thinking is not a value-neutral activity. The methodology is impacted significantly by modernity, and Christians must think

Christianly about the process and determine the extent to which its presuppositions are compatible with a Christian worldview. See Baird and Soden, "Cartesian Values and the Critical Thinking Movement: Challenges for the Christian Scholar and Teacher," *Faculty Dialogue* 19 (1993), 77-90.

[24]I.e., they work.

[25]Cheney, "Telling the Truth," pp. 6-7.

[26]Betty Jean Craige, *Reconnection: Dualism to Holism in Literary Study* (Athens, Georgia: University of Georgia Press, 1988), p. 65. Cited by Cheney, "Telling the Truth," p. 22.

[27]MacIntyre, *Whose Justice? Which Rationality?* p. 353, cited by Lundin, p. 26.

[28]Sire, *Discipleship of the Mind*, p. 159.

[29]Unlike what often happens in society as the marginalized speak out and begin to try to implement their agenda, the diversity in the church must not further undermine its unity. The spirit that allowed the early church to function harmoniously with socio-economic diversity that ranged from slaves to the most prominent members of the community must be recovered.

[30]On this see Douglas Groothuis, "To Heaven and Back," *Christianity Today* [April 3, 1995], pp. 39-42).

[31]Lundin, *Cultures of Interpretation*, pp. 222-23.

[32]See Douglas Jackson, "The Rise of Evangelical Hermeneutical Pluralism," *Christian Scholar's Review* 16 (1987), 325-35. As Jackson makes clear these evangelicals affirm that "from God's perspective all things cohere in a unity" (p. 325); and that "our inability to attain completeness or unanimity in our reading of the Bible does not imply a denial of the oneness of truth itself" (p. 334); rather it is a reflection of our finiteness and fallenness in the presence of the reality created by a perfect, all-wise and infinite God.

[33]Dallas Willard, "The Unhinging of the American Mind — Derrida as Pretext," in *European Philosophy and the American Academy*, Monist Library of Philosophy, ed. by Barry Smith. Willard is describing the effect of Hume and Kant on epistemology.

[34]It would seem that different perspectives on truth are appropriate in different disciplines. Certainly an art work or a piece of literature is true in a different sense than a medical

diagnosis. A coherence view of truth is part of the picture as well and seems especially useful in disciplines such as abstract math. Given the complexities of reality and our limited understanding of it the coherence view will often be a major component in our determination of what is true. The problem with the postmodern view is the reductionism that denies the correspondence view.

[35]The books by Tate and Osborne noted below are examples of such helpful interaction and synthesis by evangelicals.

[36]Lundin, p. 9. For a discussion of the issues and a defense of the idea, amply confirmed by the history of civilization and by personal experience, that pragmatic adequacy in communication is possible see Osborne, *The Hermeneutical Spiral*, pp. 366-415 and W. Randolph Tate, *Biblical Interpretation* (Peabody, Massachuetts: Hendrickson Publishers, 1991).

CHAPTER 5

Special Revelation

Both the Bible and human experience make it clear that people made in the image of God have significant mental and analytical abilities. The great advances in knowledge and the great artistic achievements that have characterized human history make this indisputable. It is also true that significant contributions to thought and practice are made not only by believers but also by unbelievers. The Bible affirms that people were made in God's image and given dominion over the rest of creation, and the exercise of dominion seems to presuppose that people are capable of rational thought and self-determination. While we will consider this human ability to think and interact with general revelation in chapter 8, it is sufficient at this point to simply note that people are depicted regularly in the biblical text as capable of thinking and making decisions and as responsible for the consequences of those choices. Many passages affirm the fact, obvious from observing people functioning in the world, that human beings have the capacity for reflective thought and are able to discover truth as they study their world.

General Revelation And The Limits Of Man's Knowledge

Job 28:1-11 describes the impressive accomplishments of people in mining gems and minerals from the interior of the earth. They are able to tunnel into the earth, keep the mines from being flooded with water, overcome the difficulties involved in getting into and out of the shafts and successfully bring out precious metals and valuable stones. This sort of human accomplishment is impressive and attests to man's great skill and wisdom. This description, however, is set in the context of the debate between Job and his friends about the reasons for Job's suffering. The four participants in the debate have been considering this question for twenty-five chapters, and it is clear that they have been unable to produce sufficient wisdom to answer the question. Job 28:12 asks, "Where can wisdom be found?" and the following verses indicate that such questions often cannot be answered by humans—nor can they buy such wisdom with the gems and precious metals they get from the earth. Job 28:23 affirms that this kind of wisdom belongs to God and the implication of the passage is that man will get this wisdom only if God chooses to disclose it to him. Among the major emphases of the book of Ecclesiastes is the idea that there are many things about the workings of the world and the activity of God that man cannot discover or understand. Deuteronomy 29:29 indicates that there are "secret things that belong to the Lord our God" and there are things that God has revealed to us (things he intends for us to know so that we can obey him).

Thus, even as Scripture affirms the significance of man's ability to think and discover important truths through the study of the world and society, it also recognizes limits to what people are able to discover in this way. These intellectual limits are imposed on human beings, in part, because people are limited in other, more basic ways. Passages like Job 38-41 and Isaiah 40:12-26 emphasize the difference between God's knowledge and control of creation and ours, and even though people today have a much greater comprehension of certain natural phenomena than Job and his friends, the point made by the passages still stands. As Gaede has noted,

> Limits exist which curb the knowledge-gathering capacity of the human being. Accordingly, there are some things the human being will never be able to understand or comprehend fully, simply because of his finitude^G.

> These limits are not clearly defined, however, and they do not present themselves as clear-cut boundaries beyond which one cannot go. Rather, they entail the recognition that we are not God and that we will not as finite^G beings, ever attain an understanding as complete or total as His.[1]

In addition to man's limited nature, Scripture also affirms that man's fallenness negatively impacts his understanding, especially in the moral and spiritual realms. Romans 1:18-32 describes the suppression of God's revelation in nature by fallen people. They refuse to recognize and acknowledge the God who reveals himself to all people through what he created. Instead they distort and pervert the revelation and use it as the basis for all sorts of false religions and immoral practices. Humanity's inherent resistance to God and his truth takes them down paths that appear to be *right* to them but ultimately lead to death (Prov. 14:12) and separation from God. The suppression of special revelation, then, results in spiritual death.

The Necessity For Special Revelation

Scripture (see Exod. 20:1; Deut. 29:1; 2 Tim. 3:16; Heb. 1:1-2; 2 Pet. 1:20) makes it clear that God has revealed himself to his people in a special way and has communicated to them many things that they could never discover because of their finiteness and fallenness. As Phillips and Brown point out, this revelation "assumes that God can speak and that man can understand...God has formed man with his rational and moral capabilities to understand and respond to God's revelation."[2] Fallen humanity though is characterized by an innate refusal to acknowledge God and submit to his authority over them, and thus, they normally reject God's revelation, both general and special. It is only a special work of God's Spirit that breaks down this resistance and brings a person to acknowledge the truth of God's Word.[3] Kantzer describes this as "the internal work of the Holy Spirit which enables (man) to accord to all the revelatory acts and words of God their proper significance."[4]

Forms And Messages Of Special Revelation

God's special revelation takes a variety of forms, as Hebrews 1:1-2 makes clear. It includes acts of God on behalf of his people such as those associated with the Exodus and the conquest; it includes God's direct intervention into natural processes like the confrontation between Elijah and the prophets of Baal on Mt.

Carmel (1 Kings 18:20-40) or the raising of the widow's son from the dead (1 Kings 17:17-24). Special revelation includes the messages God revealed to his servants in visions, conversations, theophanies, and so forth. The focus of God's special revelation comes in Jesus Christ, as Hebrews 1:2-3 and other passages make clear. Special revelation is much more extensive than Scripture, but the Bible occupies a unique and particularly important place in special revelation.

The Bible comes to us as a divinely inspired account of various instances of this special revelation. We know the message God communicated to the prophets and to Moses because parts of those messages were recorded by authors moved by God for the specific task of writing inspired Scripture.[5] We know the teaching of the apostles in the same way. Many acts of God are described for us in Scripture,[6] and the inspired accounts often include descriptions of what happened along with an indication of what the events mean. Thus, we are told about the events associated with the Exodus — something that historians could confirm if the right evidence became available to them, and we are also told why these events happened — God was fulfilling his promise to Abraham to deliver his descendants from bondage and return them to the land he had promised to give them. Thus, God's role in the events is explained (something a secular historian could never determine and something that most of them would refuse to accept), and the significance of God's activity is explained as well. We are told in Scripture that Christ died — again something that historians could determine, given the right evidence. Scripture also tells us the significance of his death (to atone for our sins), something entirely beyond the ability of any researcher to discover. God's special revelation also tells us about his work as creator of the universe, a fact that according to Hebrews 11:3 we know by faith.

God's special revelation tells us about parts of reality that we cannot observe and study. It affirms to us that there is a spiritual realm in addition to the physical one, a realm inhabited by demons and angels. It proclaims the fact that history is moving toward a climax determined by God. It declares the return of Christ and the establishment of his everlasting kingdom, along with the fact that personal existence continues after physical death. It discloses the significance of human beings as creatures made in God's image and their pre-eminent position with respect to the rest of creation. It reveals the fact of human sinfulness and the consequences of that sinfulness, just as it reveals how to receive God's forgiveness and live in a right relationship with him. It communicates moral principles that reflect God's truth and the way he desires his children to live. This revelation also gives to us much insight into how our Creator designed us to function as human beings.

The Role Of Scripture In Christian Thinking

Special revelation is essential in integration[G] in order to refine and correct perceptions from general revelation[G]. The Bible's description of all people as sinners (e.g., Jer. 17:9; Rom. 3:23) stands as a necessary corrective to humanistic views of human behavior that, while providing helpful insight into how and why people behave as they do, fails to recognize man's fallenness. The truth found in various rationalistic and naturalistic views of the world must be supplemented by the Bible's teaching about the spiritual realm (e.g., the existence of demons or the fact of immortality).

The crucial importance of the Bible in understanding reality and thinking Christianly does not come just from the fact that it provides us with much information that we are unable to discover through observation and reason though obviously that is important. The unique value of Scripture comes from the fact that it contains information that the believing community has by faith acknowledged as having its ultimate origin with God himself. Therefore, the message is not distorted by faulty perception or interpretations of the events and realities it describes. God is not limited in his experience or perceptual ability as we are and thus can speak apart from the limits that characterize people. While it is important to recognize that inerrancy and infallibility cannot be attributed to human interpretations of Scripture, it is still important to recognize that the facts Scripture reveals can be taken as absolute truth in a way that human perception and interpretation cannot.

In thinking about the vital role of the Bible in integrating faith and learning, it is important to keep in mind certain things about this revelation. For example, it is focused in its purpose, and its intended purpose is not to tell us everything about every subject; nor is it even meant to tell us everything we would like to know about God and theology. First Corinthians 13:12 makes it clear that our understanding (even with inspired Scripture) is only partial. As we noted above, Deuteronomy 29:29 refers to secret things (things that God has not chosen to reveal to human beings); Job 28:12-28 makes the same point as do Ecclesiastes 3:11 and Romans 11:33-35. John explains that he has not presented everything that Jesus did in the Gospel account (John 21:25); rather he selected certain incidents that would contribute to his purpose of bringing people who read the gospel to faith in the Messiah (20:30-31). God's Word provides us with true truth but not with fully comprehensive truth, and it is truth that witnesses to Jesus as the Christ. It is a redemptive message and the material included was selected in order to redeem, not to fully inform. Scripture is also meant to reveal to God's people what they need to know in order to become mature believers equipped for effective ministry (2 Tim. 3:15).

Evangelicals have rather consistently affirmed that God's Word is true and without error (that is, it is infallible and inerrant), but it is important to be aware of certain characteristics of the inspired record. Scripture is both the Word of God and the product of human authors. Often theologians speak of this as a mystery not unlike the Incarnation. There the human and divine natures of Christ come together in such a way that they cannot be separated. In just the same way the human authors wrote the divinely inspired message in language that reflects all the characteristics of their own background, education and experience. As Pinnock suggests, "The sacred writers retain their individuality...The Spirit accommodates himself to the manner of men's speaking...The human (authors) made use of the full range of their human capacities. No single psychological experience was common to all the sacred writers."[7] The message is communicated in human language and follows the normal rules of that system of communication. Proper interpretation must recognize the kind of literature, the historical and cultural context and a variety of similar factors.

As Pinnock has noted, the evangelical claim that in the original autographs the Bible is without error has to do with the intended assertions of Scripture, and "it is sometimes necessary to distinguish the <u>subjects</u> (e.g., creation and God's sovereign control of the universe) Scripture teaches from the <u>terms</u> (e.g., the four corners of the earth, the pillars of the earth, etc.) employed to discuss them."[8]

It is important to recognize certain important characteristics of biblical language[9] and thought.

Five Characteristics Of Biblical Language

1. It is **popular rather than scientific language**.

Biblical language is the language in which people converse. It is the language of the marketplace, of social gatherings, the language used in daily conversation. It is not the technical language of the university or of any scientific or theological discipline. God's Word is directed to his people, not to some elite group of scholars among them. The prophets' sermons were often delivered to the masses (e.g., Jer. 7:1; 36:4-6), and Paul's letters were directed to the churches rather than to a highly educated leadership. The message was intended to convey God's truth to those who heard it, and this would require language that was understandable to ordinary people unschooled in the technicalities of theology, philosophy or science. Not only was the message meant for the common people of each author's day but it was intended by God to communicate his truth to his people over a long period of time during which there would be changing ideas about science, philosophy, etc. Accurate communication of the truth in popular language effectively accomplishes this mission. The modern reader should not try to read the Bible as if it were a modern science or philosophy textbook.

2. It is **phenomenological language**.

Biblical language is **the language of appearances**. When we talk about the sun rising and setting or we talk about the four corners of the earth, we are simply describing the way things appear to a human observer. Scripture uses this kind of language. Such language has a significant advantage over technical language because scientific theory and terminology frequently change; the appearance of things remains the same. This kind of language ensures that the message of Scripture is timeless. It should also be noted that such descriptions are just as true as technical scientific ones. The statement that an apple is red is just as true as a description of the precise way in which the apple's skin alters light before reflecting it into the human eye. Often the biblical authors present their descriptions in poetic language which takes it even further from the technical and scientific.

3. It is generally **non-postulational language**.

The other side of the coin of the previous point is that the Bible uses the language of description rather than theory. Biblical language usually does not theorize as to the basic nature of things. There is no theory of matter apart from the fact that it is real because God created it. There is no theory of astronomy or gravitation or personality taught in the Bible. Rather, the inspired writers accurately describe what they see. In discussions of people the terminology and descriptions relate, for the most part, not to the technical but to the descriptive. For example, there is no word in either the Old Testament or the New for the brain, and its crucial role in human thought and behavior is never mentioned. The cognitive function of humans is often recognized, but it is associated with the spirit, the heart, the mind, and so forth. The term *heart* refers not to some specific faculty of a person but rather to the central core of a person that controls thought, feeling, behavior and just about anything else that a person might do. The connection between thinking and behaving is recognized and meditation is seen as an important tool in changing attitudes and behavior. These points are made, however, from a descriptive perspective rather than a theoretical one.

4. Biblical language **reflects the culture of the times in which it was written**.

Reflecting the culture of the times does not mean, however, that the Bible is filled with errors and mistakes of the primitive people who wrote Scripture and thus contains numerous scientific mistakes that modern thinking must correct. The biblical message is devoid of the mythology that was characteristic of the cultures all around Israel, and this is essential in protecting the truth and accuracy of the message.

The psychological terms used in Scripture are those of the ancient world rather than those of modern science, but their accuracy is in no way undermined by that fact. Again, terms are descriptive. Emotional and psychological responses are often associated with parts of the body physically affected by the emotion. Emotions are associated with the heart, the kidneys, the liver, the bowels. Discouragement is described in terms of a fallen face; being brought out of that state is described as the face being lifted or the head being lifted.[10] Anger is described by a Hebrew idiom that literally means "the nose burns against someone." These are accurate and insightful descriptions of emotional and psychological responses, but they are descriptive rather than technical and scientific. Description does not make them less accurate; it only makes them different in intent.

We often do the same thing. An athlete of limited physical ability who succeeds beyond what one might expect is sometimes described as accomplishing what he or she does on *guts*. We understand by that description that the player has an internal drive and determination that motivates him or her to perform beyond what would normally be expected. A psychologist or academician would describe that same attribute in terms other than *guts*, but a more technical description would be no more true or accurate.

The degree of precision intended by the biblical text is determined by the original language and cultural milieu. The Hebrew word meaning *son* has a much broader semantic range than our English word *son*. It can mean *grandson* or refer to direct descendants even farther removed; in some instances it can refer to members of a group with no blood relationship to a person. The meaning of the word in the biblical text must be established from the perspective of the original author rather than that of the modern English reader. Measurements of time, distance, money, etc. reflect the limits of measuring techniques and the requirements of the society and cannot be judged on the basis of modern possibilities and expectations.

5. The language of Scripture is **consistent with its pragmatic perspective**.

The perspective of Scripture is not generally the perspective of Western formal logic where ideas build linearly on one another. Rather, it frequently associates related things/ideas together,[11] and often in different ways than we might. Most of us would recognize a clear distinction between seeing and providing; they are two separate and distinct ideas. Practically speaking, there is a connection between the activities in that an awareness of a need usually precedes actually providing for that need. Some pragmatists among us might argue that there is a practical contradiction in being aware of someone's need and then ignoring it (e.g., James 2:14-16), and the Bible (especially the Old Testament) views the matter this way.

The Hebrew word that means *see* also means *provide* in certain contexts. In Genesis 22, the account of the sacrifice of Isaac, this Hebrew word is consistently translated *provide*. The idea behind this association is a practical one and comes from the pragmatic outlook that refuses to separate theory from practice. A genuine awareness of a need (i.e., seeing it) ought to produce a practical response that attempts to meet the need (i.e., providing).[12] In exactly the same way a verb meaning *to visit or pay attention to* is often used in the meaning *to judge or to bless*. The association is that God pays attention to a person or nation and then acts in a just and appropriate way (with judgment or blessing) depending on what his examination reveals. Thus, thinking or seeing or examining are practically connected with action in a way that is often foreign to Western thinking.

Hebrew does not have a word that carries only the meaning *to obey*. The word that serves that purpose also means *to hear*. The idea reflected in this usage is that, in practical terms, it is unthinkable that a person would hear an order coming from someone in authority over them and then not do what the authority said. Therefore, no clear distinction is made in the language between hearing and obeying. They are related practically in such a way that they belong together, and a pragmatic perspective sees no need in most circumstances of technically differentiating between the ideas. This same associative thinking is seen in the functions connected with the heart in the Old Testament. Functions of feeling, thinking, memory insight and volition are seen as coming from the heart. As Wolfe says, "The Israelite finds it difficult to distinguish linguistically between 'perceiving' and 'choosing,' between 'hearing' and 'obeying.' The linguistic difficulty that ensues for our more differentiating mode of thought comes from the factual impossibility of dividing theory from practice."[13]

We can run into problems when we try to turn human language into something that it was never intended to be. Many of the ideas that biblical languages associate together linguistically are very different things to most of us, and we often make technical distinctions that, while they may be fully appropriate in systematic theology and philosophy, are not appropriate in interpreting a pragmatically oriented text. It is also possible for our distinctions to be quite pedantic and move beyond what the text intends to communicate.

Some time ago my wife called our health maintenance organization to make an appointment with a pediatrician for my son. My wife said to the appointment secretary, "We would like an appointment with Dr. Smith. He is our doctor." The nurse responded rather abruptly, "Dr. Smith is not your doctor; he is your child's doctor." She was technically correct, but given the context of the conversation, she was making a pedantic distinction that was unnecessary—and in that instance offensive. Sometimes a failure to recognize the perspective of the original author can result in the same kind of pedantic distinctions and distort the intention of the original author. It is essential to develop the kind of Spirit-illuminated common sense that allows us to know when and how far to push things like meaning of words and semantic distinctions.

Characteristics Of The Pragmatic Perspective

A pragmatic perspective is often characterized by "practical coherence rather than systematic coherence."[14] Biblical authors are generally content to identify a limited number of principles that allow them to explain or accomplish their immediate goal rather than attempting to relate that topic to others in a comprehensive system that would satisfy a modern philosopher. Many biblical passages emphasize the sovereignty of God; other passages present people's freedom to make choices and the consequences that result from those choices.[15] There are many warnings about defecting from the faith and subsequent disaster, particularly in the book of Hebrews (e.g., Heb. 3:12-4:13; 6:4-8; 10:26-39). At the same time there are many passages that teach the eternal security of the believer (e.g., John 6:35-40; Rom. 8:29-39; Jude 1:24). These two groups of scriptural passages would seem to be in conflict; the Bible gives little attention to resolving the apparent conflict in the way a Western logician would. We must not assume that one passage contains the whole counsel of God on a topic. Rather we must carefully search the Scriptures to find every emphasis that is relevant for the question we are trying to resolve, and we must also realize that all the biblical passages may still not cover every possible practical aspect of the issue.

Biblical authors did not share the modern Western sense of the importance of chronological order, and occasionally biblical narrative will depart from chronological order because the particular emphasis of the text can be better served through another order. For example, Chronicles reports David's transfer of the ark to Jerusalem as one of the first things he did on becoming king, apparently to show that proper worship of the Lord was a top priority for him. Samuel reports it later in his reign, apparently reflecting the correct chronology.

A pragmatic perspective is often satisfied with approximation rather than technical exactness because the accuracy of the point being made is not undermined by the approximation. Measurements for time, distances, and so on lack the kind of precision that would be possible today. This lack of precision does not mean that they are not true; nor does it mean that the truth of any biblical passage is compromised in any way. As Pinnock has said, "Scripture selects the degree of exactness it requires."[16] Old Testament quotes in the New Testament are sometimes inexact because the point the author wanted to make did not require an exact quote. In other instances (e.g., Matt. 22:43-46) the author's argument hinges on some detail in the Old Testament text and a more exact citation is used. Sometimes round numbers are used instead of exact ones and often numbers (particularly three, seven, ten, forty) have a symbolic significance rather than an exact significance. The number translated 10,000 comes from a Hebrew root meaning *a large number*, and that is probably what the word means in some contexts (e.g., 1 Sam. 18:7).

As was noted above, many different metaphors are used in Scripture to explain important biblical doctrines like the church and salvation. Poythress says about the biblical analogy comparing the church and the temple,

> The analogy reveals a depth dimension that transcends merely superficial comparisons. We find here multiple relationships based on the profound unity of God's wisdom for creation and redemption...when we identify a biblical saying as an analogy or a metaphor, we should remember that far from being rhetorical tricks, biblical analogies express profound truths.[17]

Such analogies seem especially well suited for expressing truth about human phenomena or spiritual realities. As Poythress suggests, "it may not be possible to capture them adequately using only one model or analogy."[18] People can often achieve useful insights through a single perspective, but "overall, they always misrepresent humanity by reducing and flattening humanity to one dimension."[19]

The Many Dimensions Of Biblical Language

An understanding of the benefits of a multidimensional approach should also enhance our appreciation for the different ways Scripture communicates truth to us. While the Bible does express truth in propositional terms (that is, in statements of fact), it also communicates it in other ways, ways evangelical scholars have sometimes failed to adequately understand and acknowledge. The language of poetry, particularly in many of the psalms, seems less designed to communicate information than to tap into the emotional aspect of human reality. The poetry reproduces in us some of the emotions of the psalmist as he struggles with difficulty and responds to it as a person of God. The emotions communicated by the literature impart to us an aspect of truth that could not be conveyed through statements alone. The early chapters of Genesis (which we will look at in a later chapter) powerfully communicate profound truths about what it means to be human, about sin, redemption, the power and wisdom and grace of God, and other subjects, but they do it through stories and images in a way quite different from the theological propositions of Paul about many of the same topics.

Old Testament narrative communicates complex truth about the realities of human experience, and this literature is well known for its lack of interpretive commentary about the events it describes.[20] Such "narrative minimalization," as Alter notes, has the effect of bringing us "to ponder unexpressed psychological depths and theological heights." These narratives also reflect the truth that "there is...something elusive, unpredictable, unresolvable about human nature."[21] The ambiguity of human experience communicated by the narrative reveals an important truth about human reality in a fallen world. Narratives such as the Joseph story and the book of Ruth effectively depict the mystery of the interaction between divine providence and human action and choice. The portrayal of mystery and ambiguity as an important part of human reality sets in clear relief the fact that the life of faith sometimes involves clinging to the promises of God in the presence of data of human experience that offers no unambiguous evidence for God's sovereign control or even of his commitment to us.

Proper interpretation of God's Word requires an understanding of the nature of biblical language; such awareness will go a long way toward keeping us from imposing modern categories on the ancient text and finding technical distinctions in the text where they do not exist. It will, as well, enable us to allow the text to more accurately teach us the exact message that God revealed through his inspired spokesmen.

Questions For Further Consideration:

1. Give examples of information revealed in Scripture that we would not know or that we could not be confident of if it were not in special revelation.

2. Can you think of a time when your opinion about some issue has been changed or modified because of your study of Scripture? How did the change of mind occur?

3. Describe one particular area where you think contemporary society has put itself at a practical disadvantage by ignoring special revelation.

4. In what specific instances does secular psychology (or sociology, or philosophy, or politics) ignore the fallenness of human beings as described in special revelation?

5. Why is it important to be aware of the characteristics of biblical language? Can you think of an instance where this understanding could help you interpret a biblical passage more accurately?

6. You are talking with a new acquaintance and happen to use the phrase *my wife* (or *my husband*). The person you are talking to interrupts you to point out that you do not own your spouse. You think about this for a moment, realizing that your critic has focused on the word *my*. You then mentally run through other uses of the word: my car, my parents, my country, my language, my name. How would you respond to your friend?

7. Read Psalm 69. Do you think the primary purpose of the psalmist is to communicate information (that is, propositional truth)? What is the psalmist communicating in the psalm? What sort of truth is communicated in the passage?

Notes

[1]S. D. Gaede, *Where Gods May Dwell* (Zondervan, 1985), pp. 50-51.

[2]Phillips and Brown, *Making Sense of Your World*, p. 82.

[3]Scripture does not always clearly indicate the extent to which man's inability to understand the truth of special revelation is an intellectual or a spiritual problem, which is perhaps another example of the pragmatic perspective that looks primarily at the bottom line. For our more precise Western way of thinking it is important to distinguish between whether the unbeliever is unable to understand or unwilling to accept the truth. From a practical perspective it doesn't really matter because the end result is the same. Passages like 1 Corinthians 1:21-25 make it clear that the message of the Cross seems foolish to people apart from a special work of God in their hearts. As Kantzer ("The Communication of Revelation," in *The Living Word*

of Revelation, ed. by Merrill C. Tenney [Grand Rapids, Michigan: Zondervan, 1968], p. 78) points out, "In the Biblical vocabulary various terms and phrases are employed to describe this work of the Spirit. Man tries or tests the spirits to discern whether they are holy. His ears are opened and he hears; scales drop from his blind eyes and he is able to see; his conscience is pressed; his heart burns within him; his mind is enlightened and the vision of God is unveiled for him." What is certain is that when a person by faith acknowledges Christ as Savior, the revelation of God in Scripture is seen in a totally different light. It no longer appears to be foolishness but is seen as God's truth which we must acknowledge and to which we must submit.

[4]Kantzer, *ibid.*, p. 77.

[5]Passages such as 2 Timothy 3:16; 2 Peter 1:20-21; Acts 1:16 clearly affirm this.

[6]For example, Creation, God's provision for his people in the desert, the defeat of Israel's enemies, God's judgment on his disobedient people, the resurrection of Christ, the expansion of the early church, etc. Salvation history psalms such as Psalms 78, 105, 106, 111 recount these acts of God and encourage reflection on them as a way to develop a greater appreciation for the power and goodness of God as well as a deeper commitment to obedience and praise.

[7]Clark Pinnock, *Biblical Revelation* (Chicago: Moody Press, 1971), p. 94.

[8]Pinnock, *ibid.*, pp. 71-72. It is sometimes difficult to distinguish between poetic and descriptive language and the author's own conception of the universe. Creation is often described so as to create a feeling of awe in the reader as he or she reflects on the majesty of the world and beyond that on the greatness of the Creator. The language that most effectively accomplishes that is not always the language that best contributes to scientific analysis.

[9]The basic points made here are suggested by Bernard Ramm, *The Christian View of Science and the Scripture* (London: The Paternoster Press, 1955), pp. 46ff.

[10]For example, Gen. 45:26-27.

[11]The early chapters of Proverbs illustrate this way of thinking. The fundamental principle of wisdom, "the Fear of the

Lord," is identified in 1:7, and then a series of examples related to the practical outworking of the principle is given in the following chapters. The result is a kind of literary or verbal collage. The pictures in the collage are related not by linear logic; rather, they are related in that they all have something in common with the Fear of the Lord idea.

[12]The point made by the use of the word in Genesis 22, of course, is that God's awareness of a need prompts him to act by providing for that need.

[13]Hans Walter Wolfe, *Anthropology of the Old Testament* (Philadelphia: Fortress Press, 1974), p. 51. Another example of this same thing is found in the Hebrew words for sin. Most of the words can mean the sin itself, the guilt that the sin produces, the punishment for the sin or the offering that was offered as forgiveness was sought.

[14]Sherwood Lingenfelter, "Formal Logic or Practical Logic: Which Should Form the Basis for Cross-cultural Theology?" a paper presented at the Consultation of Anthropologists and Theologians, Biola University, April 14-15, 1986, p. 7.

[15]For example, Genesis 49:10 ("The scepter will not depart from Judah...Until Shilo comes") seems to indicate that the royal line would be established through the tribe of Judah. First Samuel 13:13-14, though, indicates that Saul's dynasty had the potential for enduring forever and that Saul's disobedience kept that from happening. Joseph's brothers were responsible for his being sold into slavery in Egypt (Gen. 45:4-5) yet he can also say, "it was not you who sent me here but God" (45:8). In some passages the two ideas are set together with no attempt to explain how they cohere systematically. For example, in Acts 2:23 Peter tells those to whom he is preaching, "this Man, delivered up by the predetermined plan and foreknowledge of God, you nailed to a cross by the hands of godless men and put him to death" (see also Acts 4:27-28).

[16]Pinnock, *ibid.*, pp. 76-77.

[17]Poythress, *Science and Hermeneutics*, pp. 113-14.

[18]*Ibid.*, 116.

[19]*Ibid.*

[20]For example, we are not told whether the decision Abraham and Sarah made in going to Egypt to escape the

drought (Gen. 12) was right or wrong or wise or foolish. Likewise, the decisions made by the characters in the story of Jacob's tricking his father into giving him the blessing (Gen. 27) are not evaluated—the reader must do that for himself. This is quite typical of Old Testament narrative.

[21]Robert Alter, *The World of Biblical Narrative*, p. 67. He also points (*ibid.*, pp. 65-66) out that the biblical authors "were clearly writers who delighted in the art of indirection, in the possibilities of intimating depths through the mere hint of a surface feature, or through a few words fraught with implication." Such techniques for communicating truth are very different from those found in philosophical or theological propositions.

CHAPTER 6

Interpreting Special Revelation: General Considerations

Despite the ominous sound of the word, hermeneutics is something we do every day; we already know and practice many of the elements necessary for proper interpretation. By beginning with what we already know about hermeneutics, we can then move fairly easily into the minor modifications necessary for interpreting the Bible.[1] **Hermeneutics** is the science of interpretation. It is the process we use each time we interpret any document, or for that matter, something we hear. Normally though, we understand (another way of saying interpret) what we read and hear intuitively, and we seldom stop to think about what we are doing. All the steps take place in an instant in the brain, and we subconsciously process the data before us and determine what the other person means. It may be useful to consider the dynamics of communication in order to understand what happens in the process of conveying and interpreting a message.

The Process Of Communication

It cannot be said too often that communication is a complex process. It involves a dynamic relationship between a speaker and hearer or a writer and reader. The **author** produces a **text** that a **reader** then interprets, all three working together to establish the meaning of the communication. As Tate says, "The...meaning is not to be found in either world (author, text, reader) or in a marriage of any two of the worlds, but in the interplay between all three worlds."[2] The speaker wants to communicate a certain message and chooses words, phrases, and sentences to accomplish that goal. In contrast to the assumptions of radical postmodernism, our own experience and the history of civilization provide ample evidence that the communication of information can occur—if not with absolute precision, at least with enough effectiveness to get the job done most of the time. Communication also presupposes that conventions exist as to how a language works, what words mean denotatively (that is, the explicit meaning), connotatively (that is, the ideas [negative or positive] associated with the word), and affectively (that is, the emotions that the use of the word triggers), and that those who use the language accept and apply those conventions with general competence.

A number of factors do contribute to ambiguity in human communication. For example, words have a certain range of meanings, rather than a single precise and invariable meaning. If this were not the case, we would have to remember and use a vastly greater number of words than we do. The English word *bow* can be used as a verb to indicate a proper response to royalty or a response to a staggering defeat. It can have several different meanings when it is used as a noun. It can be a part of a boat or something a girl might wear in her hair or put on a package; it can denote a weapon used to shoot an arrow or a device used to produce sound from a violin. For accurate communication to occur, a reader or hearer must understand as precisely as possible what a speaker or author intends by the words, sentences, paragraphs that he or she uses.

The Importance Of Context

A communicator must, therefore, provide the necessary clues to enable a hearer to process his or her comments and determine both the exact part of each word's semantic range intended by the communicator and how the words and sentences fit together. The word *bill* in a sentence like "I saw a bill on the grass" could refer to a part of a cap, a piece of money, a document indicating the amount of money owed someone or to a part of a duck. Most of the time, we instantly understand which of these meanings the speaker intends by the way it fits into its context, the things said and done before and after it. If a teenage son has just come into the house from mowing the lawn and hears his father, who is paying the family bills, say he has misplaced the telephone bill, the father would understand immediately what the son means when he says, "I saw a bill on the grass." On the other hand, if someone had been counting paper money in the yard, the meaning would be understood differently. We see then that context contributes greatly to meaning. Apart from a context containing clues as to what the communicator means, the sentence will most likely be misunderstood. The context includes both the surrounding words, phrases and paragraphs as well as the set of circumstances out of which a discourse arises. It is the context that provides many of the clues to meaning, and **context** becomes perhaps the most important single factor in determining the meaning of a communicated message.

The speaker/author communicates a message out of his own historical and cultural setting; the way he does this reflects his own understanding of the language and his skill in using it. In 18th century England the sentence, "The apothecary went home to bring the bills," would have meant something almost no one would understand at first hearing today: that the pharmacist had gone to his home (which was also his shop) in order to pick up ("bring") certain doctor's *prescriptions* ("bills"). There are many factors that influence the speaker/writer such as his education, his emotional state, the exact task that he is trying to accomplish and his understanding of his audience. We recognize that speakers and authors do not always communicate the message they intend, and all of us have had the experience of saying or writing something that was understood by someone in a very different way than we intended. Several years ago a baseball player who often was at odds with the press, complained that the press "always reports what I say instead of what I mean." Evidently he was a better ballplayer than he was a communicator. While the competence of the communicator is often an issue in ordinary human communication, the divine inspiration of the Bible takes this variable out of the equation. We still have to deal with the intention of the author and seek as a reader to determine exactly what the text says. Nevertheless, we can at least proceed with the awareness that the message is communicated accurately.

It is important for the interpreter to understand as much as possible about the context of the communicator and his message in order to know with precision what the communicator means. Many different things constitute the context that an interpreter uses to understand a message. A headline like "Indians Slaughter Tigers" means one thing to a reader who sees it in the sports page; it would mean something quite different to a reader who saw it in the international news section. Something as simple as an awareness of a speaker's identity can sometimes be the key that allows an interpreter to establish the context so as to correctly understand an otherwise cryptic message.

On March 17 several years ago, our phone rang just as we were sending the kids out the front door to catch the school bus before it pulled away. I answered the phone and a child's voice on the other end said, "Would you ask your wife if I should take the eggs out of the refrigerator now." I had no idea what the person was talking about. I was standing in front of the refrigerator and it was just about breakfast time, but that context was not enough to allow me to decipher the communicator's message. Unable to think of anything else to do, I handed the phone to my wife, and she immediately understood the whole thing.

The person on the phone was one of my son's friends. My son collects bugs and butterflies and he had given his friend some silkworm eggs the previous fall. My wife told him to put the eggs in the refrigerator and leave them there until about St. Patrick's Day. Then he could take them out and wait for the eggs to hatch. As soon as my wife recognized Stephen's voice she understood exactly what he meant. Once I knew the context, Stephen's words made perfect sense; apart from the proper context they were ambiguous and confusing, if not totally misleading. Apart from other indicators, one would normally expect the word *eggs* to mean hen's eggs, especially when the word was set in the context of *refrigerator* and the normal time for breakfast. But my wife knew of a different context and, once she recognized who was on the phone, she was well on her way toward figuring out what this person was talking about, and a few well-chosen questions cleared up the mystery entirely.

Other Factors In Accurate Communication

Many different things, such as the type of language and the literary, historical, geographical or cultural setting, can effectively serve as clues to an author's meaning. It is essential for the communicator to provide ample clues and for the receiver of the communication to pick up on those clues if precise communication is to take place.

The precision of communication is improved when hearers/readers come out of the same historical, linguistic, cultural and experience pool. I can communicate more effectively with my wife than I can with most other people because she is able to pick up on many clues that I provide (sometimes unconsciously) because we share so many experiences and she knows me so well. We read between the lines and understand a message that is not overt in a letter or conversation. If I am talking about some technical area in biblical studies or theology, my wife might not understand me well at all while someone with whom I share a common background in those technical areas can understand me with little difficulty. Difficulty in communicating clearly with international students is greatly increased because they do not have a thorough knowledge of English and the exact semantic range of the words we are using. These difficulties are compounded by differences in cultural perspective and experience.

Another dimension of the ambiguity in communication is pointed out by Tate. He says, "Since an author employs verbal symbols in communication, and since verbal symbols carry a wide semantic range of meaning, an author quite possibly (actually quite probably) communicates much more meaning than was consciously purposed."[3] This characteristic of language sometimes gives to literature a fuller meaning that stimulates a reader to understand dimensions of an idea that the author never imagined as he or she wrote. This ambiguity occurs in Scripture as well and is particularly seen in those instances where the New Testament sees dimensions in an Old Testament passage that the original author perhaps did not fully comprehend. While this phenomenon is characteristic of language in general, it is the doctrine of inspiration that ensures that meanings exceeding those consciously intended by the author may nonetheless be a part of the Divine Author's intention. As Gabel and Wheeler put it, sometimes "what God wished to say was something more profound or far reaching than what the human author was apparently saying."[4]

It is essential to recognize the dynamics of communication, and to realize that what the author means, what the text says, and what the reader understands are vital, though not always identical, elements in the process. Linguistic, historical, cultural and experiential differences make it difficult to ever achieve exact correspondence between what the author means and what the reader understands, but the lack of *exact* correspondence does not change the fact that pragmatic adequacy in communication is possible and that effective communication does take place even across cultural and linguistic boundaries. The differences that exist between the biblical world and today, while obscuring many details, are not sufficient to prevent the adequate communication of God's truth to believers in any time or culture.

The Bible As Communication

The Reformers insisted that the Scriptures are *sufficient* and *clear,* and as Packer points out, the statement that the Scriptures are sufficient means that "They contain all things necessary for salvation and they do not need to be supplemented from any other source such as tradition, experience, etc."[5] Packer notes that the statement was never meant to suggest that the Bible tells us everything we would like to know about God and his ways or that it answers every question that it might occur to us to ask. The statement that the Scriptures are clear and interpret themselves from within means that Scripture, as God's written word, stands above both the Christian and the church and is the final authority for them both. It means, Packer says, that "The Christian using its provisions can learn all that he needs to know for his spiritual welfare. It does not mean that he can solve every problem or understand every text; rather it means that God's people will always know enough to lead them to heaven starting from where they are."[6] The Scriptures are clear and sufficient for their intended purposes, and those purposes, as we noted earlier are: "to give you the wisdom that leads to salvation" (2 Tim. 3:15) and "that the man of God may be adequate, equipped for every good work" (2 Tim. 3:17).

Biblical interpretation has numerous similarities with the interpretation of other types of communication, since God chose to reveal himself through human language, and the normal dynamics of communication operate in that special revelation. Certainly God works through his Spirit to help us understand his Word, but the basic principles of communication and interpretation are not suspended by that activity.

Difficulties In Understanding The Bible

As we think about the way communication works, several difficulties in understanding the message of the Bible suggest themselves. First of all, the Bible was written in Greek, Hebrew and Aramaic, and thus it is imperative that we, to the degree possible, accurately determine the semantic range of the original words used and the grammatical and syntactical features of the text. The culture in which God chose to reveal himself was a different one than ours, and it is essential that we try to understand as much about the culture of ancient Israel and their way of thinking as we can. We are not suggesting that a believer in North America (or any other part of the world) studying the Bible in an English translation (or any other language that the person knows) will be unable to understand it. The Word of God is still sufficient and clear in those circumstances. An awareness of geography, the languages, the historical circumstances and the culture and religion of Israel and her neighbors can make important contributions to a more precise understanding of the biblical author's message, and in certain instances it can prevent inaccurate and false interpretations. The difference, as one scholar has put it, is the difference between seeing something in black and white and seeing it in color. It is the difference between a person's understanding of New York City only from reading about it as opposed to reading that same description after having been there. It is not that one has no understanding without a knowledge of these matters; rather it is that the person has a much fuller and more accurate understanding if he or she is aware of these things.

My sons sometimes have trouble understanding the verses they memorize from the King James Bible. Words like *conversation* or *beseech* or *the froward man* conjure up images out of their experience that are very different from the meaning intended when that version was first translated in 1611. It is

101

imperative that we, as much as is possible, understand things from the perspective of the original author and not impose our own perspective onto the text and distort its intended meaning.

The Importance Of Knowing The Bible's Original Context

Osborne exhorts the interpreter to make judicious use of background information. Understanding such material is crucial because "There are 'shared assumptions' between the author and the original readers, information not found in the text, data that they knew but we do not. While semantic research and syntactical analysis can unlock the literary dimension, background study is necessary to uncover that deeper level of meaning behind the text as well as within it."[7] Background holds the potential for providing "a major access point to the historical dimension of the text. The interpreter needs to discover these underlying 'givens' for properly understanding the text."[8]

An awareness of the original context and the worldview of the original author and readers, insofar as that can be determined, allows a reader far removed from the original communication to identify certain shared worldview components that are helpful in bridging the gap between *then* and *now* in terms of both understanding and application. At the same time an awareness of worldview differences is critical if an interpreter is to read out the meaning the author intended his original audience to understand while minimizing the modern interpreter's reading meanings into the text that are peculiar to modern culture.

As Tate notes, "Behind every literary text, there lies a view of life, a view which has been conditioned by the author's real world. While an author may imagine a literary world with all sorts of new possibilities, the expression of such an imaginative world is impossible apart from the author's real world. An author can imagine a world and express it textually only through the real historical, cultural, literary, and ideological setting."[9] He further points out that "The most effective safeguard against a wholesale imposition of the interpreter's world upon the world of the text is the diligent study of the world that produced the text."[10]

The Spirit Of The Age And Interpretation

It is also easy to allow the modern zeitgeist or *spirit of the age* to become a decisive factor in our interpretation. Karl Barth, in his discussion of the image of God, showed how the prevailing interpretations of that concept over a long period of time followed almost exactly the current emphases in anthropology, sociology, psychology and other social sciences. Scholars were allowing current fashionable themes to determine how they understood a biblical idea that in its biblical context is rather ambiguous. As noted above, the same phenomenon sometimes happens in the interpretation of prophecy. Somewhat ambiguous passages are given meaning by current events until different current events require a modification of the way those passages are understood. By putting ourselves, as much as possible, into the world of the original author, we can minimize this sort of thing and improve the accuracy and consistency of our interpretation even if *more accurate* interpretation sometimes turns out to be less detailed and specific.

It occasionally happens that the point that is clear from the biblical text is a different point than we are interested in, and it is possible to miss the clear point of the text in the struggle and debate over how the details of the passage relate to the question of interest to us. The Genesis passages about man's creation in the image of God make it rather clear that the image of God gives humans a dignity and worth not shared by anything else that God created. The significance of our creation in the image of God is clear, even if exactly what in us (if anything) constitutes the image of God is quite ambiguous. It seems obvious that what is clear from the text ought to take priority over what is ambiguous, and our own emphasis in preaching and teaching ought to reflect the priorities of Scripture. It is sad when believers become so involved in debates over details of creation that we entirely miss the clear point of the biblical accounts.[11] The same can be said about a number of other theological debates that often divide the body of Christ. It is important to be aware of this danger and work to avoid the problem.

The need for understanding so many different areas of knowledge suggests the importance of utilizing those who have devoted themselves to the study of these matters. Isaac Newton is supposed to have said in reply to someone who commended him for his great scientific discoveries, "If I have seen farther than those before me, it is because I was standing on the shoulders of giants." The same principle applies in biblical studies as well. Certainly commentaries and resources of various kinds must be used with a critical eye and with an awareness of the presuppositions of those who write such commentaries. We would recognize that there is a kind of spiritual insight that is possible only for the believer, but it must also be acknowledged that information helpful in understanding various details of the biblical text does sometimes come from people who are not believers. An atheist familiar with details of the geography or history of Israel or the ancient Near East can provide far more accurate information of this sort than the most pious believer who is ignorant of such matters; even the most intense prayer and fasting will normally not overcome that ignorance—though diligent study usually will. The same is true in many other areas such as philology, grammar, literary structure and even a sense of the context in which a text occurs. As Ramm recognizes in his quote of Barrows, "The extended investigations of modern times in these departments of knowledge have shed a great light over the pages of inspiration, which no expositor who is worthy of the name will venture to neglect."[12]

A thorough knowledge of the principles of hermeneutics as important as it is will not compensate for ignorance of the language and background of the text, and hermeneutics assumes that important work of this kind has been done before interpretation of the text begins. Questions of textual criticism, along with higher critical questions such as authorship and date, must be answered, and answers to such questions can significantly influence (and even determine) certain interpretive conclusions. A basic awareness of the issues can be gleaned from a Bible dictionary or encyclopedia.

It must be emphasized that hermeneutics is both an art and a science. It is a science in that specific rules and principles must be followed, but it is also an art in that the principles must be skillfully applied to the text. There are some people, not formally trained in the principles of hermeneutics, who do quite well at interpretation; they just seem to have enough common sense to apply the right principles to the text. At the same time there are people who know all the rules, but who are not very good at interpreting Scripture. There is a world of difference between knowing all about the way pictures are painted and actually painting a masterpiece. There is also a world of difference between the technician who knows all the formulas and principles and the creative engineer who can apply principles to bring into reality a great bridge or building. As important as an understanding of hermeneutics and familiarity with the available study tools is, that knowledge alone will not make a person a good interpreter of Scripture. Becoming a skilled craftsman in interpreting God's Word takes a great deal of practice and hard work.

Requirements For Becoming A Skilled Biblical Interpreter

Some of the requirements for becoming a craftsman in the art of biblical interpretation are met in the spiritual qualifications suggested by Ramm: (1) He/she must be born again. (2) He/she must have a passion to know God's Word. (3) He/she must have a deep reverence for God.[13] I would suggest two other things that contribute as well: practice and meditation on Scripture.

Most great artists, in addition to the great amounts of time that they spend practicing their technique, diligently study their subjects and the works of the great masters. In just the same way, reflection and meditation on God's Word and his world will increase our familiarity with our subject and our intimacy with the ultimate author of the material. We gain an ability to understand the inner essence of the revelation which makes us better able to understand the correct relationships between the various parts of Scripture.

Basic Evangelical Assumptions About Scripture

As we noted earlier, the importance of presuppositions cannot be overstated, and assumptions are especially important in interpreting Scripture. Our fundamental presupposition for approaching special revelation is that Scripture is the inspired revelation of God; Scripture makes that claim for itself. We would also affirm that the Bible is inerrant.[14] It is these presuppositions that set off the grammatical historical approach used by most evangelicals from various other critical approaches. Biblical scholarship that is dominated by the worldview of modernity and naturalism[15] denies the supernatural inspiration of the Bible, significantly impacting how it is interpreted. The worldview of postmodernism also denies certain basic assumptions of orthodox Christianity such as the possibility of knowing absolute truth and the adequacy of human language for communicating truth. There are many destructive implications of such approaches, and evangelicals must part company with much of biblical scholarship at this point. Our presuppositions do significantly influence our hermeneutic, and it is essential that we remain aware of what those assumptions are.

Because we see a single divine author behind all Scripture, we will expect **harmony and consistency in the message**. We will not expect different human authors to contradict one another, so that when there is apparent contradiction we will look for some way to see harmony in the messages. We also assume there to be **a unity in the message** of Scripture, rather than seeing it as a collection of fragmented ideas that reflect the individual idiosyncrasies of the different authors. We will allow Scripture to interpret Scripture. This does not mean that we read the New Testament into every Old Testament passage that we interpret or that we assume that a word or phrase means the same thing in every passage where it is used. We still must read out the meaning of each passage and understand it in the light of its historical, cultural, and linguistic context. It does mean, however, that **what is clear in Scripture will take priority over what is obscure**. It also means that various **passages will complement one another rather than working at cross purposes**. Certainly there is great diversity in Scripture that comes from many different human authors writing out of different historical and cultural settings and addressing many different problems and doctrinal issues. At the same time there is **a coherence in the basic doctrinal teaching of the Bible**; the inspiration of the God of all truth ensures such coherence. Our interpretation of a particular passage should not contradict the overall teaching of Scripture on that point.[16]

For example, Romans 5:12-21 establishes a parallel between the work of Christ and that of Adam and describes the contrasting effects of their work on all mankind. In the discussion the words *all* and *many* are used to describe that effect. Verse 12 says that "through one man sin entered into the world, and death through sin, and so death spread to all men because all sinned." We recognize this classic statement of the universality of sin and its consequences. We read in verse 15 about the free gift which comes through the work of Christ, "much more did...the gift by the grace of the one Man, Jesus Christ, abound to many." We immediately recognize this statement as being about the grace that is made available to those who believe. However, the terms *all* and *many* are not used consistently throughout the passage; in verse 18 we read that "through one act of righteousness there resulted justification of life to all men," and in verse 19 we are told that "as through the one man's disobedience **the many** were made sinners." One could take these last two statements as *proof* of universal salvation and *limited* sinfulness of mankind. It is only because we read the verses in the light of the many passages that teach that universal salvation is not true and that universal sinfulness is a fact, that we recognize the proper way to understand the meaning of these words.

The doctrine of inspiration also means that **we accept what Scripture tells us to be historically true**, and we accept the fact of supernatural intervention into human affairs with respect to miracles. In contrast, most critical scholars see the miraculous not as what actually happened (in their view the scientific method precludes that), but rather as the interpretation of certain pious people in the religious community; they see these stories as perhaps having been believed by many and as having served a useful purpose in that they glorified God and elevated his reputation in the eyes of the people. Our presuppositions about the nature of Scripture and the activity of God in history cause us to accept the biblical statements as accurate statements of historical fact except when there are indications in the text that certain stories (e.g., parables) are simply literary devices. These are some of the ways our presuppositions influence and even determine our hermeneutic.[17]

In a sense, this interpretation is no different from what we do in interpreting other kinds of literature. If we read a legal contract that has been carefully reviewed by lawyers representing both parties in an agreement and we find things that appear to contradict, we suppose that there is something that we have not understood correctly because we know that kind of document normally does not contain contradictions. In the same way, if we receive information from a friend that appears to contradict what we know is true, we would normally (if we know our friend to be a person of integrity) try to find out what lies behind the apparent contradiction. We would assume that there was some way to resolve the tension in the information. On the basis of our friend's integrity, we would expect that there was a way to harmonize the data.

Being Aware Of Our Assumptions

It is essential to be aware of our presuppositions so that the process described above[18] for refining our worldview may be applied to our study of Scripture. We approach the text with certain assumptions about it, and we interpret the text in the light of those presuppositions and our experience (i.e., general revelation). As we interact with the data of the text, we sometimes sense a tension between the text, our assumptions about it, and general revelation. There is a dynamic relationship between assumptions, general revelation, and text with each one influencing the others to make both our interpretation and our presuppositions more accurate.

When I began working on a commentary on Song of Songs a few years ago, I approached the study with a certain understanding of the story presented in the book. The book consists of a number of poetic glimpses of the man and woman, and the interpreter must determine if there is a coherent story and then piece together what the story is. I felt comfortable with an approach that finds three major characters in the story rather than two. This approach argues that Solomon saw a beautiful young girl on one of his trips to the north and brought her to Jerusalem in order to make her his wife. He wooed her and offered her the splendors of his kingdom if she would consent to marry him; she was encouraged to accept his proposal by many others who thought such an opportunity would be the most wonderful thing that could happen to them. This girl was in love with a young shepherd boy from the north and in spite of the offers of wealth and splendor and honor and power in Solomon's court, she turned Solomon down and returned to marry her shepherd. This approach to the book solves the problem of having Solomon with his 700 wives and 300 concubines as a role model for true love. It also very powerfully shows the nature of true love which cannot be bought or coerced. A story about Solomon's unsuccessful attempt to win the love of this girl from the north would have had great appeal among those who were less than happy with the oppressive policies of Solomon that finally led to the division of the kingdom. As I studied the text with this assumption, I was troubled by the frequent necessity of having to see the girl's words or actions as part of a dream or of having her react to Solomon's words of love in similar words — but words now directed past Solomon to her absent lover (who is never explicitly identified in the text). The text forced me to refine my assumptions about the story, never an easy task, and hopefully resulted in a more accurate interpretation of the book.

It is not possible for an interpreter to come to the text apart from assumptions about that text that come out of the interpreter's worldview. As interpreters we must enter into a dialogue with the biblical text with the sort of openness that allows the text to correct us and change our assumptions even as those assumptions influence our understanding of the material. The tragedy occurs when our assumptions are so firmly established that they determine what the passage means even before we seriously interact with it in the interpretive process. Such an attitude denies the possibility that God can teach us a truth we do not already know.

Questions For Further Consideration:

1. The present author once visited a Sunday School class where the *Mizpah Blessing* ("May the Lord watch between me and thee while we are absent one from another") was used as a benediction to dismiss the class. What do the words mean in the context of dismissing a class? Look at the words in their biblical context (Gen. 31:49 — include the context of the chapter and the broader context of the Jacob and Laban story). What do the words mean in the biblical context? Do you think it is appropriate (or biblical) to use these words to dismiss a class? Why or why not?

2. Can you recall a time when you heard someone using a biblical verse out of context? What can you do to minimize this problem?

3. Describe a time when something you said was misunderstood because the person with whom you were speaking failed to understand the context of your conversation.

4. With each of the following words, give its denotative, its connotative and its affective meanings: king, kill, save, command, spiritual.

5. Choose a biblical passage that seems troubling to you. Read as much as you can about the background (historical, linguistic and cultural) of the passage. How has your study clarified the passage for you?

6. Find several biblical passages that deal with the following topics: money, warfare, animals, property. How do you think the present zeitgeist tends to obscure the original meaning of the passages?

Notes

[1] A number of excellent books on hermeneutics are available. For students at an introductory level Henrichsen and Jackson, *Studying, Interpreting and Applying Scripture* (Grand Rapids, Michigan: Zondervan, 1990); Fee and Stuart, *How to Read the Bible for All Its Worth* (Grand Rapids, Michigan: Zondervan, 1982); and R. C. Sproul, *Knowing Scripture* (InterVarsity Press, 1977) are especially helpful. For more advanced students W. R. Tate, *Biblical Interpretaion: An Integrated Approach* (Peabody, Massachuetts: Hendrickson Publishers, 1991); Bernard Ramm, *Protestant Biblical Interpretation* (Grand Rapids, Michigan: Baker Book House, 1970); and Grant Osborne, *The Hermeneutical Spiral* (Baker Book House, 1992) are excellent.

[2] Tate, *Biblical Interpretation*, p. xx.

[3] *Ibid.*, p. 5.

[4]John Gabel and Charles Wheeler, *The Bible as Literature* (Oxford: Oxford University Press, 1986), p. 256. As Derek Kidner (*Psalms 1-72* [Downers Grove, Illinois: InterVarsity Press, 1973]) points out in many instances it was the events associated with the coming of Christ that made clear what these fuller dimensions of meaning were. As he says about one passage (p. 20), "So startling an exegesis of the psalm must have been too dazzling to contemplate, until events, in the coming of Christ, accustomed the eyes of believers to the full glory of the truth."

[5]J. I. Packer, "Hermeneutics and Biblical Authority," *Themelios* 1 (1975), p. 5.

[6]*Ibid.*

[7]Osborne, *Hermeneutical Spiral*, p. 127.

[8]*Ibid.*, p. 412.

[9]Tate, *Biblical Interpretation*, p. 7.

[10]*Ibid.*, p. 27.

[11]Certainly the primary point is that God created everything that exists and that the creation reveals to us what he is like. God's power and wisdom are clearly demonstrated in what he has made.

[12]Bernard Ramm, *Protestant Biblical Interpretation*, p. 7.

[13]*Ibid.*, p. 13.

[14]For a more detailed statement as to what this means see "The Chicago Statement on Biblical Inerrancy," *Journal of the Evangelical Theological Society* 21 (1978), 289-96.

[15]See chapter 3.

[16]We do not mean to imply that the way to accomplish the internal consistency that we are claiming for Scripture will always be clear or easy to attain. There will be many places where ambiguity will remain, and for a variety of reasons. The biblical authors often addressed different questions than we do, and they provide data to answer different questions than we are asking. In some instances we can never harmonize the data because there is insufficient data to do so. The interpretive uncertainty that often attaches to difficult passages and the lack of data about certain issues will create situations where we will be unable to demonstrate how tensions in the text can be resolved in a totally convincing way.

[17]On this, see "The Chicago Statement on Biblical Hermeneutics," *Journal of the Evangelical Theological Society* 25 (1982), 397-401.

[18]See chapter 2.

CHAPTER 7

Interpreting Special Revelation: Applying The Method

The grammatical historical method[G] is the interpretive method that was practiced by the Reformers, the approach taken by most evangelicals today. This method essentially applies the same interpretive principles to the biblical text that one would apply to any human communication. The method recognizes that the original author intended to communicate a certain idea to his audience, and it seeks to understand that message in exactly the terms that the author intended. **The goal of the method is to discover the meaning and intention of the text**; the goal is exegesis[G] (that is, reading out the meaning that the author intended) rather than eisogesis[G] (that is, reading a meaning external to the text into it).

This method is sometimes called a literal hermeneutic, and by literal we mean, "the natural or usual construction and implication of a writing or expression; following the ordinary and apparent sense of words; not allegorical or metaphorical[G],"[1] The literal method fully recognizes the use of metaphors, figures of speech, symbolic language, word plays, puns, the psychological and emotional effect of certain words, etc. and attributes to these expressions the meanings and emotions that they ordinarily convey in normal communication. The method does allow for historical development of word meanings and the historical development of ideas.

Allegorical Interpretation

In contrast to the literal interpretation that characterized the Reformation and those moderns who are its heirs, the allegorical method[G] was widely practiced by both Jewish and Christian interpreters in the period prior to the Reformation. Allegory is a type of literature in which incidents and characters in one realm of experience actually represent those in a different realm of experience. Sometimes the Bible describes political and historical figures through stories that on the surface have little to do with the actual events but which clearly depict the historical reality. This kind of literature is found in the Bible in Judges 9 and Psalm 80, and in Bunyan's *Pilgrim's Progress,* a well-known extra-biblical example.

It is also possible to interpret a document allegorically even though it was not written for that purpose. Allegorical interpretation can be done in a number of ways and for a number of reasons. Allegorical interpretation was used by some Greek philosophers as they sought to make older popular Greek religious writings more acceptable to educated Greeks who would find the literal sense of the stories offensive or intellectually unacceptable. According to Carr, "These philosophers denied the historical reality and obvious teachings of the older writers.... The stories of the gods were not to be taken literally, they argued, but were only vehicles to convey the real hidden or secret meanings which the commentators knew."[2] This method was taken over by both Jewish and early Christian interpreters and was widely used in interpreting Scripture.

Philo of Alexandria used the method for much the same reason that the Greek philosophers used it; he wanted to establish the credibility of the Old Testament to Jews trained in Greek philosophy who found the literal meaning of some of the material difficult to accept. Philo, by allegorizing the text of the Hebrew Scriptures, was able to find many of the teachings of the philosophers.

An allegorizing interpretation of books like Song of Songs provided a way of reducing the erotic and sensual qualities in the book by transforming them into profound spiritual and theological truths. This approach seemed to be virtually required by most early Christian interpreters who came to their task dominated by a perspective that encouraged celibacy and monasticism as the ultimate expression of spirituality. These men found it unthinkable that the love of a man and a woman, including the physical and sexual expression of that love, could be a topic worthy of inclusion in Holy Scripture. By allegorizing the book, interpreters were able to make it into a description of the relationship between God and his people (the Jews or the church or the individual believer). As Ramm points out (p. 32), Origen found the allegorical method an effective tool for eliminating what appeared to be absurdities or contradictions in Scripture. It was also useful in making Scripture acceptable to those schooled in Greek philosophy who thought the stories in the Old Testament to be intellectually unsophisticated and inferior.

It is worth pointing out that a certain presupposition—or maybe a presumption—underlies this. The interpreter has passed judgment on the suitability of the literal or plain sense meaning of the text, deciding such a sense is inappropriate. He looks for a way out of that meaning through the allegorical method of interpretation. Certainly there are texts whose plain sense meaning we reject for whatever reason, but we must be very careful about this. Scripture is the final authority, and we must never set ourselves as the judge of God's Word. We must let Scripture speak to us and submit to what it says; we cannot be faithful disciples if we simply pick and choose those things that appeal to us or that seem logical or culturally acceptable and then eliminate the difficult teachings by our interpretive method.

The allegorical method was not used just to eliminate the plain sense meaning of problematic passages. Origen was typical of those who practiced this method of interpretation in arguing that the literal meaning of the Scripture is a preliminary meaning; it is for laymen and the immature. History is symbolical and typical, he taught, and the true disciple will seek the deeper spiritual meaning of a text. Such interpreters were convinced that the New Testament is concealed in the Old, and they believed that the only way to bring that out was to spiritualize the text. They felt compelled to read the Old Testament allegorically so that the people and actions in it meant nothing more than a spiritual lesson, ignoring more literal meanings. Origen believed that understanding the Old Testament in a literal way would leave us in Judaism. Evangelicals have generally rejected spiritualizing or allegorical interpretations of Scripture and have followed the grammatical historical method used by the Reformers. It is that method which we will now describe.

The Practice Of The Grammatical Historical Method

An important distinction must be made between three different, but related, aspects of interpretation. **Exegesis** involves reading the message that the original author of the material intended to convey to his original audience. **Synthesis** involves bringing together everything that the Bible has to say about a particular topic in order to put together a comprehensive picture of that subject. **Application** means determining how the biblical teaching, determined from exegesis, should impact believers in a historical and cultural context different from the one in which the message was originally revealed.

Exegesis: Four Steps

There are four steps in the process of exegesis: determining the context, determining the meaning of the words, making use of biblical parallels, and considering the kind of literature.

1. Determine the context

Determining the context includes, but certainly is not limited to, the literary context. Words are the basic carriers of meaning in any language, but it is words in relation to one another that convey the message. It is necessary to think in terms of phrases, sentences, paragraphs, sections, groups of sections, entire books, etc. The boundaries of the various units must be identified and a determination made of the general point the author is making. To the present writer this priority supercedes any other task of the interpreter. Perhaps the best way to determine boundaries and points in a preliminary way is to read the passage a number of times in a variety of translations. As the material is read (hopefully the entire book in most cases), the reader should pay attention to the author's argument and purposes, the way the parts of his argument fit together, the kind of logic he is using (e.g., formal vs. point), the repetition of words, themes, and so forth. As the study progresses with detailed studies of words, sentences, paragraphs, and related matters, this preliminary understanding of context will be refined, helping us to further understand the meaning of the various words and other elements. There is an interplay between such elements as the understanding of context and the meaning of words; both influence the other and work together in what might be called a kind of spiral that produces a more precise understanding of the passage.

The context also includes the author's historical and cultural context. Some of this information may be evident from simply reading the text, but normally commentaries, Bible dictionaries, history books and similar reference tools provide helpful information not apparent to the reader. A proper understanding of Isaiah 7 requires an understanding of the historical situation facing Judah and Ahaz. A knowledge of the events preceding the destruction of Jerusalem by the Babylonians is necessary for an accurate interpretation of the books of Jeremiah and Lamentations. An awareness of the conditions faced by the post-exilic community makes the preaching of Haggai and Malachi much more understandable. The more the interpreter learns of the cultural environment of the biblical author, the easier it becomes to discover that details of the text are clarified by that understanding.

2. Determine the meaning of the words

A second element in exegesis involves determining the meaning of the words used in the passage. As was noted above, a general understanding of a word's meaning will result from simply reading the passage. A good sense of a word's meaning will normally result from seeing how it is used in a particular context which normally takes priority over meanings that are suggested primarily by the etymology of a word. Words are normally used apart from any awareness of etymology (For example, both the word *sinister* and the word *gauche* etymologically mean left handed; but that is almost never a part of what is meant when the words are used today, and most people who use these words are quite unaware of their etymology). Word meanings change over time; a word that was once directly related in meaning to its etymology may take on a meaning that is only marginally related to the original meaning. It must also be kept in mind that sometimes the etymology of a word is less than certain, and scholars are not always ready to admit this possibility.

The interpreter must refine this preliminary understanding by studying the significant words in more detail. It is generally helpful to study other passages where the word is used in the Bible (and outside the Bible as well if such data is available). The use of a concordance is helpful although it is important to be sure that the passages you are comparing use the same Greek or Hebrew words since several Greek or Hebrew words will be translated by the same English word (remember each word has a range of meanings and a translator chooses the meaning that the context requires). By examining a word in several different contexts, it is usually possible to gain some understanding of the semantic range of the word, an essential step in trying to determine exactly what the word means in the passage of interest. Sometimes it is helpful to compare passages where similar ideas are discussed in order to see what words are used. Through this kind of examination it is often possible to determine whether the biblical authors use certain words consistently or whether there is flexibility in the vocabulary. As Ramm points out, "If the New Testament shows flexibility in its vocabulary then our theology ought to reflect this flexibility."[3] While every student can use the methods outlined above to learn much about what important biblical words mean, it is usually helpful to make use of Bible dictionaries and word study tools since the authors of those works are conversant with the original languages.

Words should be studied in the light of the cultural background, and an awareness of the culture can sometimes help us know how a text would have been understood by its original readers. For example, words like *image* and words having to do with occult practices and magic, will have strongly negative connotations in the Bible because the culture strongly condemned any use of images; similar words in the other Semitic languages or Egyptian will have very different connotations because images played an important role in religion and life and were viewed positively.

Since Christianity has its origins in the Judaism of the first century, the apostles and the early church saw the New Testament as a continuation and fulfillment of the Old Testament. Old Testament background of New Testament concepts should be recognized and understood. The language of the New Testament is Greek, but the thinking, the culture and the tradition are

Semitic (i.e., Hebrew and Aramaic), and this background must be understood if the New Testament is to be interpreted accurately. Some understanding of these matters comes from increasing familiarity with the Old Testament through personal study, but most will have to come through commentaries and works that treat the cultural background in some detail. Words that occur frequently or words that deal with important concepts will usually be discussed in Bible dictionaries, and in discussing the general meaning of the words, particular attention will often be directed to the cultural background in which the words were used.[4] Commentaries often provide significant information about grammar, word meanings, culture, history, and related matters; such tools can be particularly useful to students without a knowledge of the biblical languages.

3. Make use of relevant biblical parallels

A third tool that can often help in correctly interpreting a biblical passage is the use of parallel passages. It is rarely the case that a biblical author will present an exhaustive treatment of a subject in a single passage; it is important to study other passages that deal with the same issue. For example, we noted in the previous chapter that certain verses in Romans 5 could, in isolation, be interpreted in a way that supports the idea of universal salvation and limited human sinfulness. The use of other passages dealing with the same topic makes it clear that this interpretation of the verses is not correct. Parallel passages can be effectively used because of the unity and harmony of Scripture; it can be expected that the various sections will complement one another rather than conflict. Reformers inferred this important element by their well-known saying, "Scripture interprets Scripture." In making use of parallels, it is essential to determine that the passages compared actually deal with the same topic rather than simply using similar language. For example, in the next section we will point out that not all the passages that use the terms *elect* and *election* are talking about the same thing.

In using parallels it is also important to be aware of history and the idea of progressive revelation (what Walter Kaiser calls the principle of antecedent revelation). Since the purpose of exegesis is to determine what the author was saying to his audience, priority must be given to the original audience to whom he was communicating. An audience at the time of David or Moses or Isaiah was not aware of New Testament truth, and that information would not have been used by either the author or the audience in understanding the message God was revealing to them. On the other hand, David would have been aware of what Moses wrote, and he may well have assumed that his audience was familiar with the same material and would understand what he wrote in the light of that prior revelation. Antecedent revelation must be applied in doing proper exegesis while subsequent revelation can only be used with substantial justification (which will only occasionally be the case).

The interpreter dealing with the statement, "You have made him a little lower than 'Elohim'" in Psalm 8:5 should distinguish between what the text meant to the original hearer (that is, what it means in its Old Testament context) and how the New Testament uses the words in Hebrews 2:7. Exegesis of the Psalms passage should focus on what the words mean in its Old Testament context, while exegesis of the Hebrews passage should focus on the meaning in the New Testament context and on how the author of Hebrews is using the older material. The discussion and application of the Psalms text is not done in a vacuum that excludes the additional revelation that has come since David wrote the psalm, but proper exegesis cannot suppose that David was aware of the later use of the material. The same is true of the comments of Psalm 8 about man's dominion which are applied to Christ by both Paul and the author of Hebrews. The interpreter should separate the question of what the text meant to its original audience from the question of how the New Testament uses the material. In some instances the New Testament authors provided an interpretive commentary on the text; in other cases they simply applied the principle contained in the Old Testament passage to the new (and sometimes very different) context being confronted; in still other instances the New Testament finds quite unexpected meanings that are possible only because the life, death and resurrection of Christ have made those meanings possible, giving them a context unavailable to the Old Testament author, though clearly intended by God. The interpreter should first address the question of what the text means in its original context before considering the question of how the passage is used in the New Testament. Certainly the New Testament can influence the interpretation, and the principle of harmony will ensure that there not be conflicts between the meaning in the Old Testament context and the New Testament use; there must be an organic connection between the two.

An Example Of The Use Of Biblical Parallels: The Concept Of Election

A study of the biblical concept of election requires an examination of each passage where the various forms of the words translated *elect, chosen, selected* are used. In addition, other related words such as foreknowledge and predestination must be studied. This study makes it clear that not every text where one of these words is used deals with the same thing. A distinction must be made between the passages where God is the subject of the electing/choosing and where man is the subject. It becomes clear, as well, that there are several different categories even when it is God who is doing the electing. There are elect angels (1 Tim. 5:21), and these appear to have nothing to do with election of people for salvation. There is election for service (1 Sam. 10:24; Deut. 18:5; John 6:70, etc.), and while normally God chooses saved people for service, there is no certainty that this is always the case and these passages belong in a different category than those dealing with election for salvation. The election of Christ is mentioned in several passages (e.g., Matt. 12:18; Isa. 42:1; 1 Pet. 2:4, 6), and again it is clear that this is not election for salvation (though there may well be some relationship between the two categories). The election of Israel, which is different from election for salvation, is mentioned in passages like Deuteronomy 4:37 and Deuteronomy 7:6-8. The election of Israel was corporate and did not guarantee the salvation of any individual member of the group. This election was certainly a gracious choice of God (Deut. 7:6-8), and it appears to have been a sovereign choice as well. Finally, passages like Ephesians 1:4 and 2 Thessalonians 2:13 make it clear that there is such a thing as election for salvation.

In addition to categorizing all the passages that use words related to *elect*, there are a number of passages that seem to be related thematically even though they do not contain the actual terms. Some of these passages include John 17 where Jesus speaks of those whom the Father has given Him out of the world; Acts 13:48 which speaks of those responding to the Gospel who were "appointed unto eternal life"; and Revelation 17:8, 20:15 and 21:27 which talk about those whose names were (or weren't) written in the Book of Life from before the foundations of the world. The use of parallel passages requires a careful assessment of the relevance of each parallel in terms of both similarities and differences. In the case of the biblical idea of election, Paul seems to include three of these categories (election of Israel, election for service and election for salvation) in his important discussion in Romans 9-11, and at points he seems to merge the various categories together. While this merging does not reduce the difficulty of exegeting that passage, it illustrates both the legitimacy of using parallels and that one cannot simply assume that every biblical mention of election refers to the same thing. Perhaps the most important thing to remember in using parallel passages is to determine correctly how the passages are alike, how they are different, and what legitimate relationships exist between the parallel passages.

4. Consider the kind of literature

One important aspect of interpreting both verbal and written communication involves the awareness that there are different types of literature (or genres), each with its own set of characteristics. We recognize that a fairy tale is different from a legal contract, that a love song is different than a personal letter or a political speech. We also understand that a correct understanding of the communication must take into account the characteristics of that particular type of communication. The same is true in interpreting the Bible. There are a number of different kinds of literature in the Bible (e.g., proverbs, poetry, law codes, parables, historical narrative), and proper interpretation must reflect the characteristics of the type being considered.

While the discussion between Job and his friends certainly is not about literary genre, one part of their misunderstanding came about because they failed to recognize the type of communication Job was using. Job's friends responded to the news about the disaster that had befallen him by traveling some distance to be with their friend. They were shocked to discover the intensity of Job's suffering, and they sat with him silently for seven days before anyone said a word. It was Job who began the conversation in chapter 3 by cursing the day of his birth and wishing that he had never been born. Job's friends were shocked by his words because they expected a man of Job's great wisdom and piety to respond in a different way than Job had. Eliphaz responded to Job with a mild rebuke that continued to escalate as the friends continued their attempt to *correct* their wayward brother. Job responded to them in chapter 6 by conceding that his words had been rash. He disputed, however, the interpretation they had given his words. They assumed that Job was expressing theology by his words; Job argued that his words, admittedly rash words, reflected not his theology but the extent of his pain. Job said in 6:26, "Do you intend to reprove my words, when the words of one in despair belong to the wind?" Job's point was that *cries of pain* need to be interpreted differently from *theological discourse*. It is vitally important both in our biblical interpretation and in our conversations with our friends to recognize the genre of the communication in order to avoid the kind of harmful misinterpretation practiced by Job's friends.

While there are a number of different kinds of literature found in Scripture,[5] we will mention only two to illustrate the point. A parable is a story or illustration taken from nature or life, often to teach a moral or spiritual lesson. While some extended parables are similar to allegories in that several elements in the parable represent aspects of the truth being conveyed (e.g., the parable of the sower), generally a parable intends to teach one central truth. As Ramm points out, "The typical parable presents one single point of comparison."[6] To interpret a parable as if it were an allegory[G] where every element corresponds to some reality in the spiritual realm is misdirected.

A proverb is a short, catchy saying that expresses a general truth. Someone has defined it as "The wisdom of many; the wit of one." As Sproul says, "[Proverbs] reflect principles of wisdom for godly living. They do not reflect moral laws that are to be applied absolutely to every conceivable life situation."[7] It has been said that a proverb captures a tiny cross-section of truth, and thus many of those cross-sections will have to be put together to produce a somewhat comprehensive understanding of a topic. Because proverbs state general truths, they are very different from absolute laws to which there are never exceptions. Often proverbs appear to contradict one another (e.g., "Look before you leap" and "He who hesitates is lost"). The same situation is found in the Bible as Proverbs 26:4 tell us not to answer a fool according to his folly while 26:5 tells us to answer a fool according to his folly. Putting the two proverbs together makes the point that in certain situations the wise thing to do is to challenge a fool, perhaps even using his own methods against him, while in other situations the right response is to ignore the fool or at least to avoid responding to the fool using his same kind of foolishness.

Understanding the characteristics of a proverb is essential in avoiding the sorts of misunderstandings often encountered in the church (e.g., taking the warnings against co-signing a loan as an absolute prohibition). It is also important in avoiding the disappointment that can result from assuming that each proverb is an invariable promise of God (e.g., "Train up a child in the way he should go, and when he is old he will not depart from it").

Synthesis

As was noted above, Scripture normally does not present everything it teaches about a topic in a single text. Rather, relevant comments about the issue must be identified throughout Scripture, brought together, and organized to produce the most complete understanding possible about the issue. This process of gathering all the relevant data and putting it together with the passage we are studying is the process we are calling synthesis. According to Packer,

> Exegesis means bringing out of the text all that it contains of the thoughts, attitudes, assumptions, and so forth—in short, the whole expressed mind—of the human writer...
>
> Synthesis means...the process of gathering up, and surveying in historically integrated form, the fruits of exegesis.[8]

Synthesis can be done because of the divine authorship of Scripture and the harmony that is ensured. It is at the heart of the theologian's work, and it also plays a very important role in preaching and teaching. The well-known Reformation statement that "Scripture interprets Scripture" does not mean that history and progressive revelation can be disregarded as this part of the interpretive task is done. Even though God is the ultimate author of Scripture, he still chose to reveal himself to man progressively, in stages, which helps determine how the revelation would have been understood by those to whom it was initially revealed.

Another principle of great importance in synthesis is that the interpretation should always prefer a clear passage over an unclear one, and major doctrine should never be built on passages of uncertain interpretation. Finally, in the process of synthesis it is sometimes necessary to use logic to move beyond the explicit data of Scripture (often what distinguishes Systematic Theology from Biblical Theology) in filling in various details relative to a topic. A fully legitimate process, it is important to recognize when it has been done and to distinguish between (a) the explicit teaching of Scripture and (b) that which we conclude as a result of our interpretation of the biblical data or our logical extrapolations from it. It is the biblical data which is inerrant, not our theological systems, and it is important that we not confuse the two.

Application

The third and last aspect of interpretation (and in some ways the most important element) is application. The purpose of Scripture is to change our everyday thinking and behavior, not to produce a cognitive awareness unrelated to life. Application is a major goal toward which the exegetical process must be moving, and it must be a major focus of our preaching and teaching. Application is also the part of the process where the greatest disagreement exists among Evangelicals. Careful exegesis is the only correct starting point for application, which involves the transfer of the basic principles revealed in the text to the new historical and cultural setting in which we find ourselves. In addition to a correct understanding of the text, proper application requires a correct understanding of reality, particularly as it relates to people and society. Application then, perhaps to an even greater extent than either exegesis or synthesis, requires the integration of faith and learning, meaning that the person who is a skilled craftsman in application will also be an astute student of human behavior. Since each individual's experiences are limited to his own circumstances, it is important to learn as much as possible from the experience and study of others.

Synthesis also plays an important role in application. The authors of Scripture had no obligation to present the whole counsel of God each time a topic was discussed. A proper balance in application requires an understanding of the overall teaching of the Bible about the matter. Many discussions of Matthew 18 and the need for confrontation present the principles as if that constituted everything the Bible teaches about the subject even though the book of Proverbs also has much to say about the proper response to an insult or offense. The impression is given that believers have an obligation to confront anyone who offends them, and significant damage has been done to the church and to relationships because people have irresponsibly confronted others when the principles of Proverbs to overlook an insult or not to answer a fool should have been applied instead.

In the same way people often teach about responding to tragedy or suffering as if Paul's comments in Philippians 4:4 or Ephesians 5:20 represented the total biblical teaching when passages like Psalms 37, 44 and 73 and the book of Job make significant contributions to the subject as well. Believers who respond initially like Job or the author of Psalm 44 are made to feel that their response is somehow sub-Christian, and thus their pain is compounded by guilt over their supposed lack of spiritual maturity. Balance in application is at least as important as balance in other areas, and synthesis in interpretation is an essential element in accomplishing balance.

Different Levels Of Application

It is often important in application to recognize that there are different levels of application. Jack Kuhatschek suggests that these levels are like a pyramid. At the base of the pyramid are specific commands given to people in a certain set of historical and cultural circumstances. Sometimes those regulations seem far removed from our circumstances, and thus the commands seem irrelevant to us. For example, it has been some time since anyone has invited me to go eat meat that has been offered to idols; nor am I often tempted to muzzle my ox while it is threshing grain—especially since I have neither an ox nor grain to harvest. As Kuhatchek notes, the instructions of the pyramid are based on more general principles as we move toward the top.[9] The passage in 1 Corinthians 8 that warns about eating meat offered to idols clearly illustrates this idea. The command not to eat the meat is a specific application for that time and place, and it is based on the more general principle that we should not use our freedom in a way that becomes a stumbling block to a weaker brother or sister. That principle, in turn, is based on the still more general principle that we should only do those things that build others up in love. Thinking about the commandment in this way causes us to realize that there are many ways to avoid causing others to stumble and to build up others in love besides refusing to eat meat that has been offered to idols.

G. J. Wenham gives another example of the same idea. According to Deuteronomy 22:8, "When you build a new house, you shall make a parapet (i.e., a wall or railing) for your roof, that you may not bring bloodguilt on your house if anyone falls from it." Wenham suggests that this law is actually based on the sixth commandment, "You shall not kill." As he notes,

In the Near East, where flat-roofed houses are common and may be used for sleeping and sunbathing, it was a sensible precaution to have parapets to prevent people from falling off....It tells the Christian to think about the danger points in his home. To ignore them is to break the sixth command-ment by omission, if not by commission. Safety measures are more than humane: they are the will of God.[10]

By regularly moving up and down the pyramid it is possible to better understand the principles on which the specific commands are based, and at the same time to begin to realize numerous ways to put into practice those principles in our time and place.

Finally, application, perhaps to a greater degree than either exegesis or synthesis, is an art, and one must be a true craftsman to do it well. Synthesizing requires practice, practice and more practice, and it requires deliberate, conscious attention to application. Again, the meditation on Scripture to which Psalm 1 attributes the success of the blessed person contributes immensely to effective application. Regular reflection on, and delight in, God's truth makes us aware of the various dimensions and implications of that instruction and alerts us to opportunities for application. One must look for opportunities to apply the principles and then regularly evaluate and analyze our response to situations (much as an athlete reviews game films or an artist reflects on past performances) in order to determine how effective we have been in applying God's truth to life. We need to regularly consider whether the application of different principles in the situation might have produced results that would have been more desirable and honoring to God. Just as diligence contributes to success in other areas, so diligence in application will make one a better craftsman in appropriately matching the principles of Scripture to the infinite variety and complexity of specific circumstances that confront people in the real world.

Questions For Further Consideration:

1. Imagine that you are reading an eyewitness account of a major battle of World War II and that you decide to read it as an allegory. What might your interpretation of the passage be like? How close do you think your interpretation would be to what actually happened or to the intention of the author who wrote the account?

2. Would it make a difference in your interpretation of Proverbs 22:6 whether it is a proverb or an invariable law or a promise? How would an understanding that Proverbs 31:10-31 is an extended proverb affect your understanding and application of the passage?

3. Read 1 Corinthians 8. Can you see different levels of application in the passage? How might moving up and down the application pyramid from concrete to abstract and back again be useful in applying God's Word appropriately to life?

4. Pick a brief biblical passage for study and go through the four steps of exegesis mentioned in this chapter. First, determine the context, then find the meaning of the key words used in the passage, next note other biblical parallels, and finally consider the

kind of literature and the characteristics of that genre. Keep a written record of your findings. Now put your passage through the process of synthesis. What have you learned that might not be obvious to a person who just read the words of the passage? Apply the passage to your own historical and cultural situation. How do the processes of exegesis and synthesis affect the outcome of this final step?

Notes

[1]Ramm, *Protestant Biblical Interpretation*, p. 119.

[2]Carr, *Song of Songs*, Tyndale Old Testament Commentary, p. 22.

[3]Ramm, *Protestant Biblical Interpretation*, p. 13.

[4]An excellent example of the kind of study that is needed is found in Leon Morris, *The Atonement* (Downers Grove, Illinois: InterVarsity Press, 1983). Morris discusses the Old Testament background on which the New Testament builds its doctrine of the Atonement of Christ. Another useful tool for finding helpful cultural information is Craig Keener, *The IVP Bible Background Commentary: New Testament* (Downers Grove, Illinois: InterVarsity Press, 1994).

[5]Helpful discussions of different types of literature and how they should be interpreted can be found in most books on hermeneutics. A particularly helpful discussion can be found in Fee and Stuart, *How to Read the Bible for All Its Worth* (Grand Rapids, Michigan: Zondervan, 1982). For discussions of the characteristics of various types of literature found in the Old Testament, see Sandy, D. Brent, and Ronald Giese, Jr., eds. *Cracking Old Testament Codes* (Nashville, Tennessee: Broadman & Holman, 1995).

[6]Ramm, *Protestant Biblical Interpretation*, p. 283.

[7]R. C. Sproul, *Knowing Scripture* (Downers Grove, Illinois: InterVarsity Press, 1977), p. 89.

[8]Packer, "Hermeneutics and Biblical Authority," p. 6.

[9]He suggests (*Taking the Guesswork out of Applying the Bible* [InterVarsity Press, 1990], pp. 51-63) that this idea lies behind the answer Jesus gave to the scribes who questioned him about the greatest commandment (Matt. 22:36-44). He simply took them to

the top of the pyramid and indicated that all the law is captured in two general principles — love God and love your fellow man.

[10]G. J. Wenham, *The Book of Leviticus*, The New International Commentary on the Old Testament, Eerdmans, 1979, p. 35.

CHAPTER 8

The Importance Of General Revelation

As important as special revelation is for the believer, it is clear that it does not inform us about every aspect of reality. Experience makes this apparent just as Scripture affirms the conclusion. Even the life of Christ is dealt with in limited summary according to John (20:30-31), and many things are not reported, apparently, because they were not necessary to accomplish the purpose for which John (and other biblical authors) wrote inspired Scripture (20:31). Nothing about DNA or nuclear fusion is found in Scripture, yet few would deny that those constitute part of reality. Paul's statement in 2 Timothy 3:15-16 as to the purpose for which Scripture was written suggests that God never intended to explain all of reality in his revealed Word. Such passages as John 14:16-25; 15:26; 16:5-15, which talk about the Holy Spirit guiding us to all truth, are references not to all of reality, but specifically to redemptive and spiritual truth.

The history of civilization provides overwhelming evidence of the ability of human beings to discover and learn significant things by carefully studying the world. The great monuments of ancient civilizations, the discovery of writing, the development of formal principles of logic, impressive advances in science, engineering, and medicine, great masterpieces of art and literature are but a few of the accomplishments that attest to people's capacity for insightful discovery. The biblical authors observed that people are able to learn significant and practical truth from studying the world around them, and they simply assumed the general accuracy of such observations. They were quite aware of important limitations imposed on the perceptual ability of every human being because of our finiteness and fallenness, but people's ability to discover truth through their sense and reason was taken as a given by the inspired biblical authors.

Wisdom And The Importance Of General Revelation

The wisdom of Egypt is acknowledged in Isaiah 19:11-13; that of the Edomites in Jeremiah 49:7, Obadiah 8 and perhaps also in the book of Job (the events take place outside Israel [probably in Edom] and involve non-Israelites);[1] the wisdom of the Phoenicians is spoken of in Ezekiel 28:3-5 and Zechariah 9:2; that of the Persians is mentioned in Esther 1:13 and 6:13; while the wisdom of the Babylonians is referred to in Daniel 2:12-13 and 5:7. The remarkable achievements produced by human wisdom are acknowledged in Job 28:1-11, and Genesis 4 mentions several individuals associated with the discovery/invention of various arts of civilization. Apart from instances where wisdom is viewed negatively because of its connection with arrogant pride or divination and magic,[2] the wisdom of these pagan nations is recognized and acknowledged as legitimate. The wisdom of Solomon is compared with that of the *sons of the east* (perhaps Edom) and Egypt (1 Kings 4:29-34), in order to impress the readers with the fact that Solomon's wisdom surpassed that of people with long-standing reputations for wisdom.

When Israel's wisdom literature is compared with that of Mesopotamia and Egypt, it is evident that there are similarities in both form and content.[3] A comparison of the proverbial traditions of Israel with those of Mesopotamia, Egypt and many other cultures with no historical contact with Israel — and thus no possibility that their proverbs were borrowed from Israel — makes it clear that the insights captured in canonical proverbs were not unique to the biblical authors. Some of the truth contained in that part of inspired Scripture was also recognized by other people at various times and in a wide variety of cultural contexts.[4] Many of the proverbs articulate principles that can be identified by any insightful person who carefully observes the world and human behavior. It does not require special revelation to realize the benefits of diligence and the way that virtue contributes to a person's success; the same is true of the problems that a bad temper creates for an individual or the consequences that result from rash judgments and commitments.

While Scripture regularly recognizes God as the source of wisdom,[5] Isaiah 28:23-29 suggests that some of this wisdom comes from God in what appears to us to be a secondary sense. The farmer's knowledge of when and how to plant, cultivate, and harvest crops is said to come from God (vv. 26 and 29). This knowledge, though, comes not as the result of special revelation from God. Rather, the farmer learns from the agricultural traditions of his family and community. In addition he experiments with various techniques to supplement and refine the methods recognized as effective by past generations. Occasionally, a creative and innovative farmer will come up with a significant improvement on the traditional methods which ultimately will become a new basis for the tradition. Faith (knowledge based on the word of those who are trustworthy), empirical[G] observation and creative reason all play a role in the discovery and development of this wisdom that is said to come from God. The process implied by Isaiah appears to be quite similar to that by which people discover truth as they study creation (what we are calling general revelation).[6]

General Revelation And Old Testament Wisdom Literature

Scripture, especially the Old Testament wisdom literature, contains a number of examples of truth that may well have resulted from such insightful reflection on the world and life, suggesting that, in this material at least,[7] the mechanism of inspiration may have involved the filtering and selecting of people's observations, observations that were both true and appropriate for God's intended purpose. If this mechanism is correct, it provides important validation both of the principles themselves and of man's ability to discern truth. As Goldingay says,

> Wisdom reminds us that man's creatureliness is an abiding feature of him, and one of positive significance. Man is not just "lost," and the world is not just the sphere of Satan's activity. Man in the world is given life by God and called to live in accordance with his nature as God's creature, with the nature of the world as God's creation, and with the nature of

his experience as God's gift. The wisdom tradition assumes that, living in and confronted by God's world, man as man is in the presence of and confronted by God himself. Inanimate nature, worldly experience, human reasoning, all reveal something of the truth of God in regard to man and the world.[8]

The fact that many of the proverbs seem to come out of careful reflection by insightful individuals perhaps implies something else about the importance of general revelation as well. It is a well-known fact that the topics that are a major focus in the wisdom material are generally non-theological in nature. Instead, they come out of the daily experience of people and for the most part deal with areas of life that are not emphasized in the law and the prophets. Kidner says, "There are details of character small enough to escape the mesh of the law and the broadsides of the prophets, and yet decisive in personal dealings. Proverbs moves in this realm, asking what a person is like to live with or employ."[9] Murphy says, "There were other areas of life not really touched by the decalogue [that is, the ten commandments]: personal diligence, self-control, attitudes toward the poor, pride, trust in one's judgment, etc. In short the development of responsible character, over and above the goals of the decalogue, forms the heart of wisdom teaching."[10] The inclusion of such truth in Scripture may well be intended as both an encouragement and an exhortation to diligence in discovering the truth that is to be found in the world, motivating believers to gain understanding in many similar areas not directly addressed in Scripture, yet important in living effectively as the people of God.

Scripture Assumes Human Ability To Discover Truth

The biblical authors assume that people are able to discover truth by thinking about the world without trying to justify that ability. The theological basis for man's discovery of truth seems to rest in part on the doctrine of creation. The order that God built into and maintains in the universe[11] gives an important basis for studying the world and is a necessary prerequisite for discovering truth through such a process. An awareness of this order enables a person to live in harmony with those principles and contributes to his or her success. Much of the Old Testament wisdom material reflects man's search for that order. The doctrine of creation serves as the theological basis for the assumption that there is a unity of truth in the created world.[12]

The idea that people are capable of discovering truth in the world and society also reflects the fact that people are created in the image of God. While there is little in the biblical texts to explicitly tie the image of God with rational ability, there is general agreement among scholars that this is part of what it means to be made in the image of God.[13] Adam is given dominion over the rest of creation, and most assume that the image of God equips people for that task; it implies the ability to understand the world and to make decisions in exercising dominion. Adam's rational ability is reflected in his naming the animals (Gen. 2:19), in his awareness that none of the animals would meet the need for a suitable companion (Gen. 2:20) and in his recognition that the woman God made would, in fact, meet that need (Gen. 2:23). Again, the way humans are depicted throughout the Old and New Testaments reflects their ability to perceive truth as they study and reflect on their world. Men and women are regularly portrayed in the biblical text as capable of making decisions and as responsible for the courses they determine to pursue.[14]

Old Testament wisdom literature recognizes the necessity and importance of carefully and diligently studying the world and society to identify and utilize principles that contribute to success in life. The numerous proverbs that compare the sluggard with the wise/diligent person emphasize that diligence is essential for success in life. Proverbs 2 affirms the importance of diligently seeking wisdom, and the whole context of Proverbs makes it clear that *wisdom*[15] includes more than what is included in special revelation. By making people in his image, God has given them the ability to perceive some of the order he created in the world, and it appears that God expects human beings to search for that truth. Walter Kaiser suggests that the search for truth and the order that exists in the world reflects an innate desire on the part of people to discover how things work in the world. Kaiser, based on his interpretation of Ecclesiastes 3:11, says that man has

A deep-seated desire, a compulsive drive, because man is made in the image of God to appreciate the beauty of the world (on an aesthetic level); to know the character, composition and meaning of the world (on an academic and philosophical level); and to discern its purpose and destiny (on a theological level)....Man has an inborn inquisitiveness and capacity to learn how everything in his experience can be integrated to make a whole."[16]

God does not reveal to us how to build an earthquake-proof bridge or information about the moons of Neptune or the psychological effect of child abuse on people or how language works. The most concerted prayer and fasting will normally not produce such knowledge, but careful observation and diligent research will often generate an understanding of those things.

Human Ability To Discover Truth Despite The Fall

In general, the human ability to discover truth through the use of our perceptual and rational abilities is a topic to which theologians have given little attention, though the point has been consistently affirmed, if only out of empirical necessity. Human ability to discover truth in science, to express the true and the beautiful through the arts and to understand some degree of moral and ethical truth has been explained variously by different theological traditions,[17] but few have denied that people, both saved and unsaved, have the ability to accomplish such things. Calvin, while emphasizing human depravity and inability to contribute anything to one's own salvation, acknowledged that people in general are able to discover truth through reason and study. Calvin said, "In reading profane [i.e., non-Christian] authors, the admirable light of truth in them should remind us, that the human mind, however much fallen and perverted from its original integrity, is still adorned and invested with admirable gifts from its Creator." He goes on to list the virtues of pagan philosophers, rhetoricians, medical experts, mathematicians and poets and concludes, "Therefore, since it is manifest that men whom the Scriptures term natural, are so acute and clear-sighted in the investigation of inferior things, their example should teach us how many gifts the Lord left in possession of human nature, notwithstanding its having been despoiled of the true good."[18] Wilhoit quotes Calvin's commentary on Titus,

> They are superstitious who dare not borrow anything from profane writers. For since all truth is from God, if anything has been aptly or truly said by those who have not piety, it ought not to be repudiated, for it came from God. Since then, all things are of God, why is it not right to refer to his glory whatever can properly be applied to that.[19]

The Role Of General Revelation In Understanding Reality

While both experience and Scripture make it clear that human beings can discover from general revelation truth that can bring significant benefits to humanity, history attests to the difficulty in defining the exact role of general revelation in comprehending reality. As we noted earlier, modernity[G] made two very significant contributions to our understanding. First of all, it made it clear that the human capacity to discover truth goes far beyond what the church had supposed prior to the Enlightenment. As Shapiro puts it, "Christendom was obliged to deal with the dangerous notion that man was competent, by reason of his senses, to discover his own truth, and again and again that truth appeared to contradict Holy Writ."[20] Out of this awareness some concluded that human reasoning and discovery was the final authority and that Scripture was nothing more than the superstitious speculations of religious people. Such conclusions led some to imagine that people, given enough time, would discover explanations for everything. This led to a *logical positivism* which argued that any truth claim not based on empirical proof was unverifiable and therefore meaningless. For example, value judgments were dismissed since they could not be supported by observable data. Modernity impacted the church in that some applied its methods to the study of the Bible and theology so as to conform them to the prevailing scientific and historical notions of the day. The result was a denial of the supernatural. While Evangelicals concluded that too much was at stake to accept the new model, the unbounded optimism in human reason and discovery led some in Christendom to develop a worldview that was essentially a reflection of the secular society in which it existed.

Others, however, remained confident that the revelatory claims of the Bible were true and concluded that the problem lay in inaccurate, and sometimes injudicious, interpretations of Scripture. They responded to the tension created between faith and reason by looking more carefully at the Bible in order to understand its message with greater accuracy. The goal of such an approach was an understanding that harmonized the data of both special and general revelation.

A second positive contribution of modernity lay in its emphasis on the importance of careful, critical thinking; it argued that conclusions (including interpretations of the Bible) must be based on evidence and logic. The tension created in biblical studies and theology by the growing knowledge coming from the study of general revelation caused some interpreters who remained committed to the divine inspiration of Scripture to recognize that greater care was needed in reaching conclusions about the Bible and theology. These interpreters tried to glean from modernity both information and methods that would contribute to a more accurate understanding of reality.

Others saw this accommodation not as a move toward greater accuracy in understanding the Bible, but rather as a compromise that appeared to destroy the very foundations of the faith. These people more and more isolated themselves from dialogue with secular views and from the study of general revelation.[21] They took the arrogance and hubris of those committed to rationalism as evidence of the depravity of those practicing its methods and saw those opinions that were destructive to biblical faith and morality as conclusive proof that the diligent study of general revelation involved more risk than potential benefit; such study was not encouraged. Clearly, the Old Testament presents an integrated picture of general and special revelation and encourages diligence in studying creation and life to discover significant things that we will not know any other way.

The Value Of General Revelation

As we noted above, knowledge of language, culture and history is important in correctly interpreting special revelation;

these aspects of general revelation provide the context for under-standing special revelation and at many points give meaning to it. God chose to reveal himself to people through the medium of human language. The way language works, the meanings of words and the way they relate to one another to convey mean-ing, is a part of general revelation. Many important biblical con-cepts such as redemption, covenant, and sacrifice derive their meaning in special revelation from the culture, and thus general revelation. The legitimate role of general revelation in interpret-ing special revelation should be recognized by every interpreter of Scripture, and our awareness of human limits in interpreting both general and special revelation should make us aware of the dangers of dogmatism. The lessons of history (the church's response to Copernicus and other instances where the church has been forced to change its position based on knowledge gained through general revelation) should make us diligent in seeking knowledge from general revelation in order to under-stand God's truth more accurately, and they should keep us open to every helpful contribution no matter what its source. As David Diehl has pointed out,

> What infuriates the scientist is when a well-substantiated scientific view is rejected by theologians because they cannot square it with their concept of Biblical authority and iner-rancy. Of course the theologian has the right to criticize questionable presuppositions that may have crept into the inductive process of the scientist's theorizing. But there are some views that have been unpopular with theologians to which scientists have clung tenaciously not so much because of any metaphysical bias but because such views have been so superior to any alternative explanations of the data that it would be truly unscientific (and unfair to general revelation) to reject them. Some of these views have eventually forced stubborn theologians to rethink their positions—for example, the Copernican view of the solar system.[22]

General revelation also gives us knowledge about many matters that special revelation does not address, but that are, nonetheless, important for life. Normally even those most skepti-cal of the benefits of knowledge gained through general revela-tion readily accept discoveries in areas that clearly lie outside the parameters of special revelation. The Bible has little or nothing to say about water purification or nutrition or how to find a vaccination for some disease or the benefits of exercise. The knowledge of how to build a bridge or a building that will withstand the hazards of the environment in a particular area is not addressed in Scripture and few would question the accuracy or the appropriateness of such truth from general revelation. In fact, while the Bible's very existence depends upon the ability to read, it does not teach reading. Advances in medicine and technology often contribute significantly to life and illustrate some of the benefits to be gained from general revelation. An awareness of how people learn or the way chemical imbalances in the body affect behavior and emotions can be very important for life, and even those who are most skeptical and fearful of knowledge that comes to us independently of special revelation would not normally question the relevance or value of such information.

The Arts As An Aspect Of General Revelation

The arts also contribute to our understanding of reality. As Ryken points out, the arts show us that we must "reject the utilitarian mindset that scorns aesthetic form and beauty."[23] God created a world filled with beauty and color and texture and variety, and he created people with the capacity to appreciate some of that beauty. Surely the ability to enjoy the beautiful must constitute an important part of what it means to be human, and, as Ryken points out, the color and smell of a rose are not irrelevant or illusory. The arts are a "balance to the technological world that values only what is utilitarian."[24] Literature allows us to enter into experiences that we could not have, and that sometimes we would not want to experience. Literature allows us to experience the pain and reality of racism even if we have never personally been victimized in that way. Literature allows us to feel vicariously the horror and injustice of war or the nobility of sacrificing oneself for another. As Ryken points out, the arts present reality in a unique way. He says,

> The arts are never a mere copy of life. They are always a distillation of some aspect of reality. Artists use techniques of omission, selectivity, etc. to heighten our perception of some

aspect of life....The arts "distort" reality in order to increase our awareness of it.[25]

The fine arts in general — music, painting, sculpture and literature — have (until the artistic revolution called Modernism of the early 20th century) included both pleasure and instruction.[26] That is to say, a particular painting of a 14th century duke can, at one and the same time, be beautifully patterned, gorgeously colored and startlingly realistic, while it also reveals the lip and eye of a cruel man whose power over people has given free reign to his cruelty. The observer can enjoy the esthetics of such a painting while being cautioned by it — warned perhaps about allowing other people too much power, or maybe alerted to one's own weakness. Literature can perform similar functions, with the beauty of language (when patterned in appealing ways) and images delighting the reader while the lesson goes home. Robert Browning's dramatic monologue "My Last Duchess" is a good example. This view of literature as comprised of delight and instruction was the standard view from Roman times (and Horace's "The Art of Poetry") through most of the 19th century.

In the early 20th century, T. S. Eliot took this view one step further in saying the delight or pleasure was a mere distraction designed to hold the reader's attention while the message, or advice, did its work. The artist dangles a pretty bait before our noses while, around our backsides, we are being injected with an antibiotic. Such trickery does not describe well the joy most accomplished artists feel in creating their works of art. Handel, in writing the *Messiah*; Milton, in writing *Paradise Lost*; and Michelangelo, in sculpting his Moses, all showed every sign of a sincere and complete immersion in the beauty of the art they were creating.

There is then something in art beyond mere candy-coated advice. An examination of classical music, painting and literature will reveal a single principle underlying all: order behind apparent disorder. The epics of Homer, the plays of Sophocles, the symphonies of Beethoven, the toccatas of Bach, and the landscapes of El Greco at first glance all give the impression of a realistic and natural disorder, just one thing after another in no particular pattern. When looked at in their completeness — after we have read the entire epic or heard the entire symphony — we begin to perceive an overall design. We see then, as we could not

141

see when we were in the middle of the play, that even when we thought we were caught up in a chaos of events, just pebbles tossed by a haphazard ocean, there really was a mind in control of those events, shaping and directing them.

It is most probably this principle of all accomplished art, the principle of order within apparent disorder, that has endeared it to human beings throughout history. There has always, even in ancient times, existed the temptation to see events as pure chance. In the 4th century B.C. Greek tragedy, *Oedipus Tyrannos*, King Oedipus' wife Jocasta tells him, "Mortals have no need to fear [prophecies] when chance reigns supreme."[27] She believes in chance because she disbelieves in prophecy; prophecy requires an order in events, a supernatural order. She continues (as so many do) to pray to the gods for their aid in her catastrophe, but she does not believe in their power to enforce an order in human life. She would, in fact, like to go on living a life of incest, denying a moral order in the universe. She is the Greek parallel to the Hebrew referred to in Psalms 14 and 53: "The fool has said in his heart, 'There is no God.'"

Art can renew our eyes, allowing us to see beyond the distracting and confusing surfaces of life. It is difficult—nearly impossible at times—to truly believe that the world is in God's hands. When a career is shattered unjustly, or a family watches helplessly as a child dies, or a civilization decays from within, we begin to wonder whether life makes any sense after all. Art can reassure us then, as Psalm 22 did Jesus on the cross, that the design is there, even if we can almost never see that design while we are in the midst of it. In the end, when we have finished the novel, we will see that the plot was in capable hands, and we will understand how important a part of the plot every chapter was. Art is an important part of general revelation; it can tell us that, even if we don't have a firm grasp on the truth at this moment, the truth is there, just as the sun continues shining despite the clouds that block our view.

General Revelation As A Supplement To Special Revelation

Often general revelation supplements special revelation and provides the basis for more accurate and balanced interpretations of the biblical data. In both interpreting and applying the

Bible, availing ourselves of knowledge that can be learned from general revelation is essential, bringing better balance to our understanding. For example, since the Bible describes some aberrant human behavior as the result of demonic activity (Matt. 8:28-34), many believers once assumed that demons must be the cause of all mental illness. General revelation has made it clear that many forms of mental illness have organic causes, and the result has been a much more balanced (and accurate) understanding of such problems. Such knowledge has contributed significantly toward finding appropriate and effective treatments and has helped to eliminate some of the abuse that once characterized the treatment of such individuals.

The Bible addresses the question of parenting and discipline, but the biblical teaching is less than comprehensive. We are told that as parents we are to discipline our children and we are told as fathers that we are not to provoke our children to anger (Eph. 6:4), but we are not given specifics as to how that is supposed to be carried out. Research on the effect of certain approaches to discipline and information about how children learn and develop can be quite helpful to a parent who wants to be wise and honor God. Often general revelation brings better balance to our application and makes it easier to see certain points that are at least implied in some of the biblical injunctions.

For example, the Hebrew word often translated *discipline* has a range of meanings and is applied to a variety of different techniques. In Deuteronomy 8:4 we are told that God's gracious provision for his people in the wilderness was a part of discipline. In Proverbs 24:30-34 the example of the sluggard's field overgrown with weeds and not producing crops is all that is needed to discipline the wise man who walks away from seeing the example aware of the connection between the sluggard's behavior and the consequences, causing the wise person to resolve to avoid such behavior. Proverbs 29:19 suggests that words can function as a means of discipline, though it recognizes that words will sometimes be ineffective, and other proverbs indicate that corporal punishment is sometimes necessary to accomplish the goal of discipline. Thus, a wide range of methods are included in what the Bible denotes as discipline. Job 33:17 suggests that the purpose of discipline is to "turn man aside from his conduct and keep man back from pride." The goal of discipline ought to be to turn people aside from undesirable behavior and attitudes. The methods for accomplishing this are quite varied. If God is seen as the model for how discipline should be handled, it appears that he uses the least severe method necessary for accomplishing his objective. It is only when more gentle methods are ineffective that God uses more severe ones.

For the present author it was only the experience of raising children, observing others raise their kids, reading material about effective parenting, and learning much from my wife's experiences as an elementary school teacher that allowed me to begin to see the pattern reflected in the biblical material in its fuller dimensions. Sometimes discussions of parenting that claim to be based *only on the Bible* appear to be lacking in the common sense and wisdom that general revelation brings—and is meant to bring to the subject. A study of the wisdom literature suggests that special revelation provides a number of general exhortations about a topic that are then supposed to be implemented in the light of common sense and the understanding that comes from general revelation.

Almost exclusive attention to passages that emphasize the sinfulness of people and their inability to save themselves can generate the impression that people are worthless and without any value whatever, a conclusion quite incompatible with the fact that all people are made in the image of God. General revelation has recognized that many factors in our culture are damaging people's perception of themselves.[28] This recognition has put pressure on theologians to present the biblical teaching about depravity in a more balanced way, a way that also makes clear people's worth as image bearers and as people for whom God was willing to send his only son to die. As Alister McGrath has put it, "There is a real need to develop authentically Christian understandings of self-esteem that challenge the secular view of self-sufficiency and affirm our dependence on God—without destroying a person's self-worth in the presence of God."[29]

Passages like Ephesians 5:20 or 1 Thessalonians 5:18 that exhort us to rejoice and give thanks in every circumstance must be balanced by the examples found in certain psalms or in Job or in Jeremiah 20:14-18 where saints cry out to God in their pain and boldly express to him their frustration and distress. I spent a number of years in a church that taught only the New Testament part of the special revelation—or at least that is the only part of the teaching that registered with me. I was quite content with that message until I found myself in circumstances that forced me to struggle with some situations that did not appear to be working the way I thought things were supposed to work for people who were trying to do God's will. As a result of those experiences (general revelation) the material from Psalms and Job and Jeremiah and Ecclesiastes began to register with me, and the result was a more balanced understanding of the teaching of Scripture. I finally realized that often our response to difficulty and tragedy is a process; at the beginning of the process people typically cry out in their pain as Job and Jeremiah did. As the process continues believers often reach the point where truth about the importance of giving thanks and reflecting on other realities about God can be incorporated into their response.

Job As An Example Of The Role Of Experience In Knowing Truth

As we have noted, Scripture reveals to us **true truth** about every subject it addresses, but it often does not reveal to us **comprehensive truth** about those matters. Sometimes experience can be a legitimate (and necessary) way to supplement the true truth revealed in the Bible. An example of this, which shows that the possibilities for discovery from experience may be very great indeed, is found in the biblical book of Job. The book of Job involves the attempt of Job and his friends to explain the reason for his suffering. All the men begin with the wisdom doctrine of retribution which says that a person is blessed in proportion to his righteousness and punished in proportion to his wickedness, an idea that seems to flow naturally from the idea that God is just and sovereign over the affairs of men. Both Job and his friends then seek to apply the principle to Job's case. As a result the friends insist that Job must be wicked, otherwise this suffering would not have come on him. As Job struggles to identify sins that might have brought on his suffering, he is unable to determine what those might be, and his friends are unable to point out such sins. As Job becomes more and more convinced that he is innocent of sins of such magnitude as to account for his suffering, theological possibilities arise that are disconcerting for

Job. When Job reflects on the doctrine of retribution in the light of his innocence, it suggests the possibility that God is unjust.

Job's friends understand the implications of his claim of innocence, and they know that it is not acceptable to conclude that God is unjust. So they try to protect the integrity of their theological system by becoming even more insistent that Job must be a great sinner. Part of Job's struggle came from the theological dilemma caused by his awareness that he was innocent: he was unable to accept the obvious conclusion (that God was unjust) and yet he could not see how the problem could be resolved (apart from discovering some hidden sin that he might have committed). As Job struggled to come up with creative alternatives to the obvious conclusion that God is unjust, he suggested the possibility that his vindication might come after death (Job 14:7-22; 19:23-29). As Job demanded the right to argue his case before God himself, he realized the futility of such an encounter and perceived that a mediator or advocate would be needed in such a situation (16:18-22). Job is never told why he suffered (he did not have the prologue as we do), and the *answer* that Job is finally given is not a cognitive answer. When God appeared to Job (chapters 38-41), he did not provide any information that helped Job understand why he suffered; rather the intimate knowledge of God that resulted from the theophany caused the questions about how and why he suffered to lose their significance. Job's ideas of vindication after death and the possibility of resurrection do not contribute to a solution to the theological problems raised in the book (though some of the questions are resolved for the reader by the prologue) nor do they contribute in any way to the resolution of Job's own questions. The ideas are raised as possibilities and then dropped without being either rejected or confirmed. It is only in the light of subsequent special revelation that the ideas suggested by Job are confirmed as true, and these ideas are then integrated into the solution of the problem of suffering for the Christian. In addition, Job's idea of the need for an advocate or mediator between God and man proves to be correct as affirmed by several New Testament passages (1 John 2:1). Job comes to new understandings of truth through his experience. His experience forces him to realize that there is such a thing as innocent suffering in spite of the fact that there was little place for that in his theological system prior to his ordeal.

General Revelation And The Problem Of Interpretation

While the example of Job clearly illustrates the way experience can bring people to a clearer understanding of reality, including truth about the way God works in the world, it is also important to recognize that experience, especially individual experience, is subject to several problems that often make it a problematic indicator of *truth*. First of all, there is no guarantee that our experience is typical and indicates what others could normally expect in a similar situation. Secondly, our experiences are always subject to interpretation, and often there is great uncertainty as to the meaning and significance of our experience — as exemplified by the debate between Job and his friends.

Job's experience is in many ways unique in that special revelation interprets the meaning of Job's experience for us. While we see in Job's case the potential that exists in experience for furthering our understanding of reality, we must also acknowledge that there is often great uncertainty as to the meaning and significance of our experience and how that experience relates to other things we know. The problem of interpreting experience is further compounded by our limited perspective as we see what happens to us. (Job and his friends suffered under the same limited perspective in being totally unaware of the activities of God and Satan in these events, activities which were critically important in interpreting the events.) Accurately interpreting personal experience is also made more difficult by our own personal biases and subjectivity.

Job's friends refused to accept the possibility that he could be innocent and still suffer because such a conclusion created too much tension with their core beliefs, and acknowledging Job's innocence would have required a significant revision of their theological system. Often friends and the larger interpretive community can help us set our experience in a broader perspective and thus see more clearly how it relates to the experiences of others — as long as that community is not so committed to a certain worldview or system that they are unable to see the broader implications of the experience. The traditions of the church can also help us overcome the difficulty in interpreting personal experience because it now includes in the interpretive community believers from many different times and places. Here, as

147

well, it is important to note that the whole issue in the book of Job is the fact that Job's individual experience was needed to correct the tradition of past generations that had failed to allow the suffering of the righteous to register.

Science As General Revelation

Certainly there is a major difference between the discoveries of most academic disciplines and personal experience. Enlightenment thinking made a significant contribution when it emphasized the need for empirical evidence and critical thinking and when it affirmed the superiority of conclusions reached on that basis to those based on anecdotes and limited personal observation. In a sense the *truth* of the scientific method is often apparent in the results it produces. As Shapiro notes, "The triumph of science has been the triumph of the system of assumptions necessary in order that science be done."[30]

Different levels of certainty will, of course, be connected with different kinds of observations in the world, which should be kept in mind as we use the results of these observations in our thinking. Some principles such as laws of nature identified in the physical sciences have a fairly high degree of certainty attached to them because of the kinds and amounts of empirical data on which they rest and because of the degree to which they can be used to predict results. Often mathematical and theoretical models provide additional confirmation. In contrast, however, certain topics in both the physical and social sciences involve the study of extremely abstract and complex phenomena where there are many variables that cannot even be identified, much less controlled. Sometimes the only validation that one needs is a pragmatic one that comes from the fact that a technique or idea works. Most people who want a house built or who fly on an airplane or who go to a doctor for therapy are not interested in absolute certainty but are content with pragmatic certainty. They want to be sheltered, or fly safely, or get well.

The Hidden Assumptions In Science

Despite the impressive accomplishments of science and the progress in understanding reality to which science has contributed greatly, it is apparent that there is a much larger interpretive element in science than many suppose. The expert witnesses in court cases who present radically different opinions for the prosecution and the defense, the changing ideas about the causes of certain diseases or the hazards of eating certain foods, varying opinions about how to educate children, different recommendations about what constitutes appropriate therapy in a given instance all attest to the lack of certainty that exists among scholars with respect to the truth that is to be gleaned from general revelation.

In addition, as Poythress and others have noted, two revolutions in physics in the 20th century shattered fundamental assumptions about the nature of the universe that had dominated the scientific thinking of the 19th century. Prompted by these events Thomas Kuhn suggested a different view of how science works and significantly redefined the idea of progress in science. He argued that all scientists operate from a paradigm (a worldview) and that the paradigm creates a bias. It establishes the rules of the game for the scientist which strongly influences and sometimes determines what she looks for in research as well as how she interprets the results of her research. As Poythress summarizes the view,

> Data are never "hard facts," completely independent of any theory. What counts as data depends on...the framework of assumptions that scientists use. All data is "theory-laden." It already presupposes...that the universe is organized in a way compatible with the assumptions of science as a whole...[it] affects how scientists make observations, what they think the observations actually measure, and what kinds of data or experiments are relevant to the outstanding questions in their field.[31]

The assured results of scientific thinking are based on certain presuppositions, and they are presuppositions that cannot be proved. As Phillips and Brown point out,

<u>All</u> worldviews begin with certain assumptions and meta-physical claims....Can these assumptions be <u>proved</u>? No, but they can be demonstrated to work when they are applied to practical experience.[32]

Shapiro agrees,

<u>One is able to do science at all only if one accepts certain intrinsically unprovable postulates about the universe</u>: that a material universe exists in some meaningful sense; that the evidence of reason and our (extended) senses is sufficient to comprehend that universe; that the universe is lawful....This is a materialistic belief system, an ideology if you will, no more subject to empirical or logical validation ("proof") than any religious belief system.[33]

At the same time it must be pointed out that science is not a postmodern enterprise where rules of the game are based on blind faith or political considerations and where all the conclusions are relative. There are significant differences between the assumptions of science and those of some other systems of thought. For example, science is not based on revealed truth in the same way that religious systems claim to be. Some of the assumptions of science are self-evident and need no proof. Many of the assumptions of science are intrinsically rational which constitutes a kind of proof. In addition, these assumptions often find support from empirical evidence, and scientific theories sometimes change as empirical data makes it clear that modifications in the models are required. As Shapiro notes, a scientific theory "is not a hodgepodge of disconnected ideas; it must have internal coherence, its components must be interconnected in logical ways, as a bare minimum, they must at least be consistent with one another."

Ambiguities Of General Revelation

While we would acknowledge that truth discovered through the study of general revelation is as true as truth found in special revelation (though not necessarily as important), it is apparent that it is not easy to determine, even in the realm of science, what is fact and what is interpretation in our study of general revelation. Our perceptions of reality and our identification of the principles of order God has designed into the world (general revelation) will almost certainly include both truth and error as will our interpretations of special revelation. The reality is that interpretation and worldview play a major role in virtually everything that we do, and realizing this should go a long way toward preventing the kind of academic arrogance and pride that is often found among scholars.

The realization that our fallenness and finiteness impact us as they do and prevent us from fully understanding reality should make us even more grateful that we have access to some truth in special revelation that is truly objective and unaffected by our limited perception and interpretive capacities—knowledge that we know by faith. It is also important to note that the Bible does set some essential parameters within which the search for truth in general revelation must take place. According to Proverbs 1:7, "The fear of the Lord is the beginning of knowledge." The fear of the Lord is an attitude: it involves recognizing who God is and who we are and then living in the light of that understanding. The fear of the Lord is a worshipping submission to God and an acknowledgment of his legitimate authority over us. Our search for truth in general revelation must take place under the awareness of who God is as the creator and sustainer of all things; it must also be done in full submission to his special revelation to us. As von Rad has observed,

> The search for knowledge can go wrong because of a single mistake at the beginning. One becomes competent and expert as far as the orders in life are concerned only if one begins from knowledge about God....Israel was of the opinion that effective knowledge about God is the only thing that puts a man into a right relationship with the objects of his perception.[34]

General revelation, then, while a necessary adjunct to special revelation, always requires the disciplining insights of special revelation.

Questions For Further Consideration:

1. Consider the farmer in Isaiah 28:23-29, whose God-given knowledge of farming techniques comes through general revelation. Have you ever experienced anything similar? Have you ever learned how to do something through tradition, observation, experimentation, but believe the lessons come ultimately from God?

2. Describe what you believe to be the most important concept you have learned through general revelation, a concept that does not seem to be addressed in special revelation.

3. Describe the role one of the arts has played in your spiritual life.

4. Most Christians are comfortable using general revelation to build a house or evaluate nutrition. They are often far less comfortable using information from disciplines like psychology or anthropology (also general revelation). Why do you think this is the case?

5. Describe a time when your opinion about theology was changed because of what you learned from general revelation. Have you ever known someone who refused to acknowledge the truth of Scripture because it seemed to be at variance with their experience?

6. A friend tells you that she is struggling because her sociology (or psychology, or physics) professor is regularly saying things that conflict with her faith and, what troubles her even more, he seems to have a lot of evidence to support his claims. What advice would you give your friend?

Notes

[1]Though the theology is thoroughly consistent with that found elsewhere in the Old Testament.

[2]For example, Exodus 7:11; Isaiah 10:13 and 44:25; Jeremiah 50:35; see also the tower of Babel incident in Genesis 11:1-11 and

Nebuchadnezzar's pride resulting from his accomplishments in building the magnificent city of Babylon in Daniel 4:28-33.

[3]In general, the similarities in content occur when non-religious or nonmoral topics are dealt with.

[4]Actually the parallels between the cultures of Israel and her neighbors extend much farther than just literary forms and the content of some wisdom literature. See, for example, J. E. Jennings, "Ancient Near Eastern Religions and Biblical Interpretation," in *Interpreting the Word of God*, Festschrift in honor of Steven Barabas (Chicago: Moody Press, 1976), pp. 11-30.

[5]E.g., Exodus 28:3; 31:3, 6; 35:31; 35:35-36:2 (all referring to the skill of certain craftsmen); 1 Kings 3:4-15 (ability to govern and judge effectively); 1 Kings 5:9-14 (Eng. 4:29-34) (Solomon's literary and scientific acumen); Psalm 119:98; Job 35:11; Proverbs 2:6; Ecclesiastes 2:26 and Daniel 1:7.

[6]Our use of the term *general revelation* is different from the one normally used by theologians. Often the term is used in theology to refer to that which can be known about God from creation. We are using it in a broader sense to include all that can be known about reality from studying creation.

[7]This fact has led some to refer to the wisdom literature as *horizontal revelation* as opposed to the *vertical revelation* of the law and prophets which often seems to have come from heaven as at Mt. Sinai or in a vision as in many instances of God's revelation to the prophets.

[8]John Goldingay, "The 'Salvation History' Perspective and the 'Wisdom Perspective' Within the Context of Biblical Theology," *Evangelical Quarterly* 51 (1979), 202.

[9]Derek Kidner, *Proverbs*, Tyndale Old Testament Commentary (Downers Grove, Illinois: InterVarsity Press, 1964), p. 13.

[10]Roland Murphy, "Wisdom and Yahwism," in *No Famine in the Land: Studies in Honor of John L. McKenzie* (Claremont: Institute for Antiquity and Christianity, 1975), p. 119.

[11]For example, Genesis 1:14-19. Passages like Psalm 104 or 74:16-17 describe the world as operating according to a pattern established by God and with a coherence designed by him.

[12]Though some Christians in their desire to protect the

priority of special revelation in practice deny this point, it is an assumption that few in the Christian academic community would dispute. Since most secular academic institutions have abandoned this important principle (see e.g., David Gill, *The Opening of the Christian Mind* [Downers Grove, Illinois: InterVarsity Press, 1989], 47-61), an important and unique contribution of the Christian college/university must be to affirm this important truth. Only the Christian university is philosophically and theologically equipped to provide students with a holistic view of reality and to educate them to see the unity of truth in God's world. On this see the articles in *Faculty Dialogue* 21 (1994), and Mel R. Wilhoit, "Faith and Learning Reconsidered: The Unity of Truth," *Faculty Dialogue* 9 (Fall 1987).

[13]C. Westermann (*Genesis 1-11* [Minneapolis: Augsburg Publishing House, 1984], p. 149) says that understanding the image of God as referring to "spiritual qualities or capacities" such as memory, intellect and will "is most certainly the commonest explanation of the term."

[14]The human ability to critically evaluate options and to make decisions is clearly pictured in the early chapters of Proverbs (e.g., Prov. 4:1-6) where the child is exhorted to hold to the parents' wise instruction and then diligently apply that instruction to life with its complexities and dissenting opinions. James Sire (*Discipleship of the Mind*, p. 94) cites other examples and concludes, "the Bible itself records God speaking with such people as Moses, dealing with them in their fallen state as rational beings....Obviously, the Scriptures treat human beings as capable of understanding and as responsible for not understanding."

[15]On what the Bible means by wisdom see Curtis, "Old Testament Wisdom: A Model for Faith-Learning Integration," *Christian Scholar's Review* 15, 213-16.

[16]Walter Kaiser, *Ecclesiastes: Total Life* (Chicago: Moody Press, 1979), p. 66. Of course the section in Ecclesiastes also makes clear that finite and fallen human beings are unable to discover the work of God in the comprehensive way they desire.

[17]For a brief summary and references see Curtis, "Some Biblical Contributions to a Philosophy of Education," *Faculty Dialogue* 21 (1994), 94-96.

[18]Calvin, Institutes 2.2.15. See also 2.2.12; 2.2.18; 2.2.13-17.

[19]Calvin, Opera III cited by Mel R. Wilhoit, "Faith and Learning Reconsidered: The Unity of Truth," *Faculty Dialogue* 9 (Fall 1987), 79.

[20]Shapiro, "God and Science," p. 47.

[21]These observations were made by Dr. Bruce Narramore, "The Isolation of General and Special Revelation as the Fundamental Barrier to the Integration of Faith and Learning," presented October 22, 1984, at a President's faculty lunch at Biola University.

[22]David Diehl, "Evangelicalism and General Revelation: An Unfinished Agenda," *Journal of the Evangelical Theological Society* 30 (1987), 452. Of course, there are examples where the additional data made it clear that the church had been right all along.

[23]Leland Ryken, "The Creative Arts," in *The Making of the Christian Mind*, ed. by Arthur Holmes (InterVarsity Press), p. 115.

[24]*Ibid.*, p. 118.

[25]*Ibid.*, p. 108.

[26]For the following observations on the arts I am indebted to my friend Dr. John Brugaletta.

[27]*Oedipus Tyrranus*, Sophocles, trans. Luci Berkowitz and Theodore F. Brunner (New York: W. W. Norton), p. 22.

[28]For example, abuse, growing up in alcoholic families, the hyper-individualism and neglect that results from the breakdown of the family and community, and so forth.

[29]Alister McGrath, "Why Evangelicalism is the Future of Protestantism," *Christianity Today* (June 19, 1995), p. 23.

[30]Shapiro, "God and Science," p. 47.

[31]Poythress, *Science and Hermeneutics*, p. 44.

[32]Phillips and Brown, *Making Sense of Your World*, pp. 82-83.

[33]Shapiro, "God and Science," p. 51.

[34]Gerhard von Rad, *Wisdom in Israel* (New York: Abingdon Press, 1972), p. 67.

CHAPTER 9

Toward A Biblically Informed Worldview

As I grew up in the church, Paul's warning in Romans 12:2, "And do not be conformed to this world, but be transformed by the renewing of your mind," produced many sermons about the dangers of being influenced by the world system and the world's ways of thinking. The Evangelical cliché, "We are called to be in the world but not of it," was indelibly stamped into my mind as a warning against the inappropriate assimilation of values and opinions that are in conflict with God's truth. As my thinking about such matters has evolved (and hopefully matured a bit) over the years, I have come to understand that the issues are far more complex than I ever imagined when I heard those exhortations as a junior high and high school student. At the same time my conclusions about the importance of the basic point being made in the warnings has not been diminished by subsequent thinking. One thing that has become eminently clear in the interim, however, is the difficulty of preventing the world's values from becoming a part of the way we view the world and reality.

The Subtle Effects Of Worldly Thinking

The difficulties we face in the life of faith are often thought of in terms of the categories of world, flesh, and devil. According to Eugene Petersen,

We are, for the most part, well warned of the perils of the flesh and the wiles of the devil. Their temptations have a definable shape and maintain an historical continuity, that doesn't make them any easier to resist; it does make them easier to recognize.

The world though, is protean: each generation has the world to deal with in a new form. <u>World</u> is an atmosphere, a mood. It is nearly as hard for a sinner to recognize the world's temptations as it is for a fish to discover impurities in the water. There is a sense, a feeling that things aren't right, that the environment is not whole, but just what it is eludes analysis. We know that the spiritual atmosphere in which we live erodes faith, dissipates hope and corrupts love, but it is hard to put our finger on what is wrong.[1]

In many ways the life of the believer can be compared to navigating a boat. The destination we want to reach is God's purpose for us, and as we move toward that goal, we encounter all kinds of currents in the world. Some are helpful and move us toward the goal even more quickly; some divert us, sometimes subtly like an ebb tide at the beach, and at other times far more obviously and powerfully like a rip tide. The zeitgeist contributes significantly to these currents, and the Christian must try to use the helpful currents to full advantage while avoiding impediments that will delay him or perhaps keep him from reaching the goal at all. A careful and critical eye is needed to navigate effectively so as to identify the harmful aspects of the world and avoid the sort of conformity to the world that Paul warns against.

The Vastness And Complexity Of Reality

In addition to these difficulties, we are confronted with other realities that make the idea of developing a biblically informed worldview seem truly daunting. Reality is so vast, and the difficulties of gathering and interpreting the data of both general and special revelation seem enormous. Focusing on the legitimate uncertainties associated with interpretation and the ambiguities that life produces seems to make it impossible to develop anything resembling a biblically informed worldview. As we think about what needs to be done, we wish the task were as simple as it is for the traveler going to Alaska mentioned in the Introduction. He or she can get the weather information needed to plan appropriately from the Internet or the newspaper or any number of travel books — if only Christian thinking were so simple a task.

We know there is uncertainty and ambiguity, and there is no possibility of developing a worldview that perfectly corresponds to reality. At the same time there are many things about which Scripture is clear, and what we want to do in this final chapter is to show how those things that are clear in Scripture actually address some of the most basic worldview questions. We do not intend to develop those issues in the detail that the Bible permits; there are other books available that do that in a very useful way.[2] Instead, we want to look at the early chapters of Genesis to show how it addresses a number of fundamental issues. For the most part, we want to limit our discussion to those matters that are clear and that do not hinge on details of the original languages or sophisticated theological arguments. Despite the ambiguity and interpretive uncertainty that we must acknowledge at a number of points, it is still possible to establish many elements of a biblically informed worldview by reading the text carefully and by using the thinking tools that any serious student of Scripture brings to the task. As Packer notes,

> Evangelicals affirm that the Scriptures are <u>clear</u>, and interpret themselves from within....The ministry of the Spirit as interpreter guarantees that no Christian who uses the appointed means of grace for understanding the Bible...can fail to learn all that he needs to know for his spiritual welfare....Not that the Christian or the Church will ever know everything that Scripture contains, or solve all biblical problems, while here on earth; the point is simply that God's people will always know enough to lead them to heaven, starting from where they are.[3]

Genesis 1-5: The Clear Messages

The early chapters of Genesis have been chosen as the subject of this study for several reasons. First, the author's field is Old Testament, and personal bias, no doubt, enters into the decision. Second, there are few passages in the Bible that deal in so concise a way with such fundamentally important issues as these chapters, and one can construct a fairly solid theological foundation from these chapters (though obviously the themes must be supplemented from the rest of the Bible, and it is recognized that a number of areas of theology are not dealt with in the chapters). Third, these chapters present an important theology through stories that have a simplicity not always apparent in one of Paul's theological arguments. Despite the fact that there are many interpretive issues in these passages about which the disagreements are quite intense, there are a number of points that are clearly made and that seem to be exactly the sort of thing that should constitute core beliefs in any biblically informed worldview.

Montgomery[4] has noted a distinction that seems helpful in interpreting Scripture and incorporating ideas into our worldview based on those interpretations. He points out that a distinction must be made between the data of Scripture and the theological formulations that come out of our study of Scripture. The data are true in an absolute sense; the theological formulations cannot be held with the same degree of certainty. Montgomery also points out that there are some theological statements that are virtually certain (such as many of the doctrines contained in the creeds and confessions of the early Church; doctrines that orthodox believers have acknowledged as true through the centuries) because they are based on a great wealth of clear biblical evidence. Other theological convictions cannot be held with the same degree of certainty because there is less scriptural support for the ideas.

Our theological statements cover a continuum that ranges from those that are virtually certain (again because they are supported by much biblical data) to ideas that are quite speculative and uncertain (because there is little biblical data to support them). The way the Bible and theology inform our worldviews ought to reflect the same pattern: those things about which Scripture is overwhelmingly clear ought to be included among the core values to which we are committed, while the more uncertain and speculative concepts ought to be farther out in the worldview-web. Of course, in practice it is not always easy to tell where in the *continuum of certainty* a particular idea or interpretation belongs, though we can normally tell the difference between elements that are far from one another in the continuum. For example, the fact that Christ will return is certain, and many passages of Scripture make that clear. On the other hand, there are many details of eschatology (future things) that are much less clear because Scripture mentions those things only occasionally and then in cryptic passages.

There are intense and often divisive debates about the length of the creation days or the age of the earth or the ways and extent to which extra-biblical data can and should inform our understanding of these matters. There are debates about the historicity of the accounts and the degree to which accounts like the Fall, with its talking serpent and trees of life and knowledge of good and evil, as well as many other matters connected with the chapters, are to be understood literally. We will generally avoid these interesting and often important questions or mention them only in passing because we are convinced that these chapters contain many truths about other matters, not dependent on the answers to such questions, that are essential for a biblically informed worldview, and we want to demonstrate how this ought to work. It is our desire that every reader of this book end up pointed in the right direction as far as integrative Christian thinking is concerned. We are convinced that if this is the case, given the clarity of Scripture and the work of the Holy Spirit and the diligence of the student, other details of a biblically informed worldview will fall into place as the process continues.

Genesis 1-5 And The Modern World: A Contrast In Worldviews

It was noted earlier that matters such as authorship, date, and the cultural background of a passage are often important in establishing the context for interpreting a passage. In this particular instance, however, those issues do not seem to be decisive in understanding the basic points of this section. The more central assumption seems to be a recognition that the material is divinely inspired and thus authoritative for one's intellectual and practical life. As Blocher puts it, "We must approach the opening chapters of Genesis as inspired texts, rich with the truth of God, clothed with the authority of God."[5] The importance of accepting the material as inspired and authoritative is apparent in that while many scholars dispute whether the assertions of this chapter are true in that they actually correspond with reality, there is little question as to what the author intends by the material. As Coats indicates, "It sets out doctrine...and teaches a particular worldview."[6]

God The Creator; Man The Creature

The first verse of Genesis ("In the beginning God created the heavens and earth") declares that God exists and thus a biblically informed worldview stands in significant contrast with atheistic and naturalistic worldviews that deny God's reality or simply ignore his existence. The verse states that God created the heavens and earth, indicating that matter and energy have not existed forever as some claim. It shows that God and matter are different things, matter having been created by God, and thus affirms a reality different from pantheistic worldviews that see God in everything. The doctrine of creation is affirmed throughout Scripture (e.g., Isa. 40:25-28; John 1:3; Col. 1:16; Heb. 11:3; Rev. 4:11), and as we have noted before it is something that we know by faith. The biblical doctrine of creation focuses on what creation tells us about God. He is sovereign; God is not subject to anything; rather everything was created by him and is subject to him. The doctrine of creation makes it clear that everything that exists can be divided into two categories: Creator and created. All things owe their origin to God, including us.

As Psalm 19:1 and Romans 1:19-20 make clear, certain attributes of God are revealed in what God created, among them God's power. God's great power is demonstrated in that he speaks and things come into existence. Genesis 1 makes this point and it is affirmed many other places in Scripture. This description may, of course, not be the actual mechanism of creation, but the theological point made by the figures is clear and is found many other places in the Bible. Psalm 33:6-9, in a similar way, affirms the effortless ease with which God created, "By the word of the Lord the heavens were made, And by the breath of his mouth all their hosts" (v. 6); "He spoke, and it was done; He commanded and it stood fast" (v. 9). Job uses a different figure to make the same point. There, the creation of the sea is described in terms of the birth of a baby. God wrapped the infant sea in swaddling bands and continues to control it with the ease with which a parent controls a tiny baby.

While it is only implied in Genesis 1, other passages make it clear that God's great wisdom is also revealed in what he has created. Wisdom in the Old Testament is the ability to succeed; the ability to accomplish a goal, and God's ability to create and sustain a complex creation reveals his wisdom, as Proverbs 3:19; Proverbs 8:22-31 and Psalm 104:24 make clear. God's wisdom and power are also reflected in the order apparent in the created world as well as in his providential oversight that sustains nature and history (e.g., Ps. 147; Ps. 104; Job 36:24–41:34).

While it is not immediately apparent to the modern reader, a study of Genesis 1 in its ancient cultural setting makes it clear that Genesis 1 is lacking the mythology that was typical of the worldviews that prevailed in the ancient world and which were common among Israel's neighbors. People recognized their dependence on forces of nature such as the sun, rainfall, storms, and the sea, and their sense of dependence led them to make these natural phenomena into gods, whom they then worshipped in an attempt to appease them and gain some control over them. Genesis 1 presents the sun, the moon, the stars, the sea, and sea monsters (v. 21), not as gods who compete with the Lord, but as *things* made by the sovereign God and thus under his control. Such a perspective affirms the essential goodness of the world created by God (see Gen. 1:10; 18; 31) and allows us to take delight in nature rather than living in constant fear of it.

The biblical authors clearly see worldview implications flowing out of the doctrine of creation, and they see practical implications as well. First, as Boice notes, "When [the biblical writers] look at creation they inevitably end up praising God"[7] as Revelation 4:11 illustrates, "Worthy are You, our Lord and our God, to receive glory and honor and power; for You created all things, and because of Your will they existed, and were created." Second, reflection on creation should prompt people to stand in awe of God's great power and encourage them to trust God and his Word as Psalm 33 suggests (note especially vv. 8-12). Finally, a number of passages (e.g., Isa. 40; Jer. 10; Ps. 115 [esp. v. 15]) contrast God who created all things with idols who were made by a man's hands. These passages emphasize the absurdity of worshipping and trusting a piece of wood or stone instead of the true God. Psalm 96:4-5 shows the contrast clearly:

Great is the Lord, and greatly to be praised;
He is to be praised above all gods.
All the gods of the people are idols,[8]
But the Lord made the heavens.

What Is Man?: Toward A Biblically Informed View Of Human Beings

In addition to what Genesis 1 tells us about God and the creation in general, there are a number of things in the account that lead virtually all commentators to conclude that "With the creation of man the creation account reaches its climax."[9] The passage makes several things clear about what it means to be a human being, ideas that must be included as core beliefs in any biblically informed worldview. The first thing that is apparent is that humans are created beings. A proper understanding of personhood, a correct understanding of self, must begin with the awareness that we are creatures. We are finite, we are not God, and implicit in this idea is the fact that we are accountable to our Creator. We are not autonomous beings, and the refusal to acknowledge our dependence on God constitutes the same sinful pride that resulted in the Fall and that is the essential meaning of sin in the Bible. The fact that we are creatures has implications in terms of the appropriate focus of our trust. Just as it is absurd to trust in idols that have been made by human beings instead of trusting the God who created the world, so it makes no sense to trust man the creature instead of God the Creator. This theme is found throughout the prophets and elsewhere (e.g., Jer. 17:5-8; Prov. 3:5-8).

Even as Genesis 1 affirms that we are creatures, it also emphasizes the fact that human beings are created in the image of God. While there are many debatable issues about the image of God, as Altmann says, "Jewish and Christian exegetes will agree that in the context of Genesis, chapter 1, the [image of God] motif is to be understood as an emphatic affirmation of man's dignity and pre-eminence over the rest of creation."[10] In Genesis 1, only human beings are described using the term *image of God*, and in Genesis 9:3-6, where permission is given for people to kill animals for food, we are told that another human being is not to be murdered because that individual is made in the image of

God. As Greenberg says, "The meaning of the passage is clear enough: that man was made in the image of God...is expressive of the peculiar and supreme worth of man. Of all creatures, Genesis 1 relates, he alone possesses this attribute...conferring on him highest value."[11] The image of God in both Genesis 1 and Genesis 9 appears to be the thing that separates human beings from the rest of creation and accounts for the pre-eminent position that they occupy in the world. The dominion over the rest of creation (Gen. 1:28) that is given to people is another indication of the pre-eminent position of man relative to the rest of creation (see also Ps. 8) and implies that he is equipped with capabilities such as rational thought, moral responsibility and self-determination, abilities that allow him to function effectively in the task of exercising dominion.

Genesis 1 pictures human beings as created beings and not God. At the same time they are creatures made in God's image and they therefore have dignity and worth. This view has significant worldview implications. On the one hand, it stands in striking contrast with ancient worldviews such as that reflected in Mesopotamian myths that saw people created only to relieve the junior deities of the menial tasks of taking care of the needs of the gods by keeping up the temples and making sure that adequate offerings were brought regularly. The worldview reflected in Genesis 1 also stands in strong contrast to modern views that see humans as simply more complex and sophisticated animals but with no right to pre-eminence, dignity and worth over other living creatures (for example, the worldview of Naturalism[12]). Still more does the biblical view stand in contrast with the idea that people are nothing but biochemical organisms with neither freedom nor dignity. The biblical worldview sees humans as more than cells and tissue (Gen. 2:7 makes this clear also). They are creatures with worth and dignity because they are made in God's image, and as we noted above, Genesis 9:6 makes clear we are not to commit murder because God's image gives human beings value and significance. James 3:9 takes this idea even farther by indicating that it is totally incongruent to use the tongue to bless God and then use it to curse our fellowman who is made in the likeness (the other term used in Gen. 1:26-27) of God. People made in God's image—and that includes both men and women, all ages, races and religions—have dignity and worth, and they are to be treated (including the way we talk to them and about them) in a way that is consistent with their value. Certainly treating people as disposable things or refusing to respect them or failure to value the life of other human beings reflects a worldview fundamentally different from the one presented in Genesis 1. The lack of respect that is reflected in discrimination based on race, gender or ethnicity is incompatible with the worldview reflected in Genesis 1 as well.

Finally, one additional point can be made from Genesis 1, though it is a point that would not be apparent to a reader studying the text in a translation. The word translated *create* is recognized by virtually all scholars as a unique term in that God is always the subject of the verb in the Hebrew Bible. Some have argued that the word means *to create out of nothing*, but it is difficult to demonstrate that meaning because the word is often used almost interchangeably with another word that means *to do* or *to make*. At the same time the word describes something that God alone does, and for that reason it immediately attracts the attention of a reader. This word is used five times in Genesis 1: it is used in Genesis 1:1 of creation in general; it is used in Genesis 1:21 of the creation of conscious life (animal life as opposed to plant life); it is used three times in Genesis 1:27 of the creation of human beings. The use of the word three times in describing the creation of people powerfully affirms the point that people, made in God's image, are special creations of God. God's direct involvement in the creation of people, along with the image of God that separates human beings from everything else that was made, presents a powerful contrast to the idea that people are nothing more than the most complex and sophisticated product, so far, of a purely naturalistic evolutionary process.

Genesis 2: Human Capabilities And Needs

While there are a number of interesting observations that could be made from Genesis 2, we will note only a few of the more obvious ones. In the beginning of chapter 2 we are told that God designed and planted a garden for the man he had made and placed Adam there "to cultivate and keep it" (v. 2:15). The garden included trees that were pleasing to the sight and trees that were good for food, something that recognizes both man's capacity for appreciating beauty and God's kindness in providing for his needs, aesthetic, physical and spiritual. God issues a command to Adam in 2:16, prohibiting his eating from the tree of the knowledge of good and evil, and as many commentators point out, this says something about man. People are able to make choices; we are morally responsible creatures; we can understand and relate to God. Hoekema recognizes that the biblical view of human beings sees them as creatures and therefore completely dependent on God, yet as he notes, "Man is not only a creature...he is also a person. And to be a person means to be able to make decisions, to set goals, and to move in the direction of those goals. It means to possess freedom—at least in the sense of being able to make one's own choices....He has the power of self-determination and self-direction."[13]

An important aspect of freedom involves how man will use it in his relationship with God. Francis Schaeffer sees this as related to what Jesus (and Deut. 6:4-6) indicates is at the center of man's relationship to God: "You shall love the Lord your God with all your heart." Schaeffer points out that the love between man and God does not involve a relationship of two equals, but rather the love of the creature for the Creator. He says that such love is necessarily demonstrated by the creature's obedience. He says, "The kind of love proper here is also rooted into obedience simply because of the nature of the relationship between the two parties. Love of the creature toward the Creator must include obedience or it is meaningless."[14] He suggests that obedience to God is "the purpose of man, the only way that man can be fully human...the purpose of man—the meaning of man—is to stand in love as a creature before the Creator."[15] As man is confronted with God's command, he responds to it as a creature capable of choosing either to obey or not to obey; he is as Schaeffer puts it, "to love God, not mechanically, but by the wonder of choice. Here stands an unprogrammed part of creation—unprogrammed chemically or psychologically."[16] Love and obedience are set in clear relief by the commandment and the results, with far-reaching implications for our understanding of reality, will be seen in Genesis 3. Even if the points suggested here move beyond the exegetical implications of the verses in this chapter, the rest of Scripture makes it clear that there is justification for such conclusions.

Genesis 2 And The Human Need For Relationships

Genesis 2:18-25 makes another important point about what it means to be a human being, and again a point that should be at the center of a biblically informed worldview. God said, "It is not good for the man to be alone; I will make for him a helper suitable for him" (v. 18). The Hebrew term used here seems to refer to someone who has a strength to assist another at the point of their weakness, and a helper who corresponds to or complements the other. As the passage makes clear, Adam carries out the assignment of naming the animals with a view toward finding the suitable companion that he needs. The search was futile as verse 18 indicates, and so God designed and made the companion Adam needed. Clearly, Adam's need could only be met by another human being made in God's image, and God provided a female counterpart of the man. The passage affirms both the importance of marriage and the intimacy that is intended by God in that relationship. It is apparent that the human need for relationships is part of God's design. As Hoekema notes,

> What is being said...is that the human person is not an isolated being who is complete in himself or herself, but that he or she is a being who needs the fellowship of others, who is not complete apart from others....
>
> Man cannot be truly human apart from others. This is true even in a psychological and social sense....
>
> It is only through contacts with others that we come to know who we are and what our strengths and weaknesses are. It is only in fellowship with others that we grow and mature. It is only in partnership with others that we can fully develop our potentialities. This holds for all the human relationships in which we find ourselves: family, school, church, vocation or profession, recreational organizations, and the like.[17]

Genesis 3 And Human Sinfulness

While there are many difficult interpretive questions related to the Fall of man in Genesis 3, there are also several points made with great clarity in the chapter, beliefs that again belong in the worldview of every biblically informed believer. As most recognize, the essential point made in the section involves not the nature of the fruit, or the talking serpent and where it came from, or the meaning of the knowledge of good and evil, or any number of other intriguing questions, but the central issue has to do with the response of the creature to the Creator's instruction. In the incident described here man is confronted with God's will in clear and explicit terms and is given the opportunity to say "Yes" or "No" to God's will. As Kidner says, "As [the fruit] stood, prohibited, it presented the alternative to discipleship: to be self-made, wresting one's knowledge, satisfactions and values from the created world in defiance of the Creator."[18] The woman, and then the man, fully aware of God's word to them, are confronted by another word from the serpent, a word that contradicts God's instruction by assuring them that if they disobey God they will not experience the disastrous consequences spelled out for them by God.[19]

This incident, which defines the essence of sin, involves whether the man and woman will stand before their Creator as creatures and submit their will to the will of God. The basic issue has to do with whether they will act as autonomous beings or whether they will acknowledge God's legitimate authority over them and show their love for God by obeying his commandment. In Genesis 3 they listened to the voice of the tempter rather than to the Word of God, but the rest of Scripture makes it clear that this rebellion can take other forms as well: we can listen to others (Prov. 1:10-19; Jer. 17:5-8) or we can decide for ourselves what is good, as is described in Proverbs 3:4-8. As von Rad says about the Genesis passage, "What the serpent's insinuation means is the possibility of an extension of human existence beyond the limits set for it at creation."[20] He further describes the result of their disobedience,

> Man has stepped outside the state of dependence, he has refused obedience and willed to make himself independent. The guiding principle of his life is no longer obedience but his autonomous knowing and willing, and thus he has ceased to understand himself as creature.[21]

Scripture makes it clear that significant consequences followed Adam and Eve's disobedience. Again there are many debatable issues regarding the details of the judgment, but a number of results of the judgment are beyond dispute. First, death came into human experience as a result of God's judgment, and the rest of Scripture indicates that the death includes both spiritual death (separation from God) and physical death. Genesis 2:17 predicts the consequence and Genesis 3:19 affirms the result; throughout Genesis 5 a pattern confirms this result as each individual genealogy ends with the statement, "and he died." Romans 5 also connects physical death, in the human realm at least, with the consequences of Adam's sin.

Second, the harmonious relationship between the man and the woman was damaged as a result of the couple's disobedience. The disrupted relationship between the man and woman is suggested in that the man blames the woman for his sin, in the shame they now experience because of their nakedness (2:25 in contrast with 3:7), and in the implied judgment on the woman (3:16, "Your desire shall be for your husband; he shall rule over you.").

Third, the harmonious relationship Adam and Eve enjoyed with God was adversely affected. This is apparent in that the man and woman hid from God and experienced shame before him because of their nakedness; it is further evident as they are banished from the garden and removed from the place where they can fully enjoy the blessings God designed and desired for them.

Finally, people's relationship with nature is disrupted, and man's work becomes a difficult task rather than a joyful one. "Thorns and thistles" (3:18) represent all those elements that make man's struggle with nature a difficult one, and Romans 8:20-22 makes it clear that the effect of sin on nature and the created order was far more extensive than the brief indications in Genesis 3 suggest.

The subsequent history that follows in Genesis 4 shows that the impact of sin was not confined to the man and woman but is seen in their offspring as well. Cain, again refusing to respond in obedience to God's word to him, in anger murders his brother. Sin continues to pervade human society until sin and human rebellion cause God to punish human sinfulness by bringing the judgment of the Flood.

Genesis And A Biblically Informed Worldview

The worldview reflected in the early chapters of Genesis clearly sees human beings as uniquely endowed with dignity, honor and worth. At the same time they are creatures who experience the full meaning of human existence and enjoy the blessings that God intends for them only when they are in harmony with God's will and in obedience to his Word; it is only in that relationship that they can function as God designed them to function. When man chose to act independently of God, he, as von Rad noted above, truly "ceased to understand himself as creature." If the biblical worldview is correct in this regard, it is clear that questions like "Who am I?" and "What is the meaning of life?" can be answered only in the light of the biblical perspective. In addition, dysfunctional and disruptive interpersonal relationships and societal problems can be understood and solved (to the degree that solutions are possible) only in the light of categories such as sin and redemption.

Finally, one other important point is clear in these chapters, a point that is also essential for a biblically informed worldview. In the aftermath of Adam and Eve's disobedience and the resulting disruption of human life, God responded graciously and redemptively. The response of the man and woman was to hide from God in their shame and fear although they had attempted to solve their problem by making garments of leaves to cover their nakedness. God takes the initiative, seeks out the guilty pair, provides for their need, and graciously restores the disrupted relationship. In the aftermath of the judgment, God replaces their inadequate coverings with garments of skin. The response of God, seeking to redeem sinful people in this chapter, is illustrative of God's grace in providing for man's redemption, the central theme of the rest of Scripture.

The early chapters of Genesis, despite some significant interpretive uncertainties with respect to many details, present certain truths clearly, and these ideas must be included among the core beliefs of any worldview that claims to be biblically informed. Reality, including reality about life in a world that presently is far from *very good*, reality about what it means to be a human being and what constitutes the purpose of life and the meaning of life, cannot be adequately understood apart from biblical concepts such as Creation, the image of God, the Fall, and Redemption.

Making Progress In Christian Thinking

There are many passages that are very difficult to interpret and whose interpretations are not certain and should not be dogmatically proclaimed. At the same time there are many passages where fundamental worldview issues are taught with great clarity as was evident in our discussion of the early chapters of Genesis. We must, of course, be aware of our human propensity for carelessness in interpretation and acknowledge that we sometimes do read our preconceived notions into passages and thus fail to recognize the difference between *what the text says* and *what we think it says*. There are also many aspects of reality known through general revelation whose interpretations are less than certain. There are also things we know about reality from general revelation about which we can be fairly certain, though as we noted earlier, it is often difficult to be sure what is fact and what is interpretation.

Normally, even those Christians most skeptical about the ability of humans to discover truth (and most concerned about human wisdom contaminating truth from special revelation) readily accept truth from general revelation about how to design an automobile or build a road. The tension that exists between general and special revelation is generated where the two address the same topics such as psychology or creation. While tension is often painful, I recently heard someone say that a string that is not under tension is not good for anything. If it is under tension it can be set in motion to make a beautiful sound, or it can be used to pull something or hold it in place. A rope must be under tension to perform a useful function. Sometimes the same is true of special and general revelation. Often it is out of the tension produced when the two seem to be pulling in different directions that progress is made in understanding reality.

It is at the interface between general and special revelation, where both appear to address the same issue, that the difficult work of integration[G] and Christian thinking takes place. There must be a dialogue between the two sources, and we must be genuinely open to truth from both sources. That openness must also include the possibility that we will feel it necessary to modify our understanding of the message of special revelation at that point. We should neither be too quick to modify our interpretations of Scripture on the basis of impressive but unsubstantiated claims of general revelation, nor too quick to dismiss claims of general revelation because they create tension with our theological system. We should also learn to tolerate ambiguity, and we should have the patience to wait for more information as we seek to resolve genuine tensions that exist.

Our efforts to think Christianly must be done in the fear of the Lord, aware that we are creatures. We must bow before God's truth while we diligently seek to learn all that we can about the world he created. Psalm 1 describes a person who prospers in whatever he or she does, and while we would never suggest that the focus of the psalmist's interest is integrative thinking[22], we would argue that the success envisioned there would include right thinking about the world and life. The secret of the person's success lies in the delight he takes in God's instruction and in the fact that he meditates on that instruction day and night. Many other passages in Scripture (e.g., Josh. 1:6-9; Deut. 6:4-9; Ps. 119; Prov. 4) recognize the importance of meditative reflection on God's truth which seems to be one of the principal ways God's truth is written into the tablets of the heart as Proverbs 3:3 encourages. Through this important way, the believer follows Paul's exhortation to renew the mind in Romans 12:3.

Christian thinking involves careful and diligent discipline as the believer seeks to critically evaluate all the information that general and special revelation brings him or her. At the same time Christian thinking is sometimes as much an art as it is a science, and as Montgomery has indicated, a theologian (even a nonprofessional one) needs to work in the way a scientist works, carefully processing and organizing data; but a theologian also needs to work in the way an artist works, feeling and relating to the material in a more subjective way that allows personal interaction with the material. Such reflection helps the believer develop the kind of individual sensitivity that is needed for effective Christian thinking. As Montgomery suggests,

> Just as...the sensitive literary critic has no doubt as to Milton's stature among epic poets, so the Christian who is in

tune with Scripture can readily distinguish between theological theorizing that cuts to the heart of Biblical revelation and theological theories that (scientifically correct as they may be) operate on a superficial level.[23]

Regular meditation on God's truth helps immensely in cultivating that artistic sensitivity that is crucial in effective Christian thinking.

We have suggested throughout this book that Christian thinking requires diligence and conscious effort on our part; Christian thinking is not the result of just letting things happen. One of my students recently pointed out though that Christian thinking is much like driving a car. He said,

> When I first learned how to drive, I was frightened by the micromanagement of the driving environment. Every movement was deliberate, double-checked and (to some extent) clumsily executed. Eventually, I learned to relax behind the wheel, to absorb all the required information by scanning the road and the rear-view mirrors. Driving became a safety-oriented, relatively routine and comfortable exercise.[24]

Christian thinking works much the same way. In the beginning you decide that this is a skill that you want to develop and you give conscious attention to developing the techniques and practicing the disciplines that are required for the task. Eventually, however, Christian thinking is not difficult. You still have to exercise discipline and appropriate cautions, but it is not an exhausting or unnatural effort. Meditating on God's truth, and regular diligence and practice in thinking Christianly can make us into craftsmen and artists who genuinely love God with our minds (Matt. 22:37) and glorify God in all that we do.

Conclusion

An accurate understanding of reality is vital for success and prosperity in living in the world, and a failure to understand reality can lead to serious problems, even disaster. Several years ago my family and I went to Lassen Volcanic National Park in northern California. I hiked to an interesting area called Bumpass Hell where there is a large area of boiling springs, mudpots and other types of hydrothermal activity. While the surface of the ground appears to be normal in much of this area, the trail through Bumpass Hell is raised above the surface of the ground because the appearance of the surface is quite deceiving. In many spots there is only a thin crust covering boiling water and mud just below the surface. Imagine the possibilities for harm for the person who did not understand the reality of the area.

Imagine the danger for a person who did not understand reality about a serious, but treatable, physical condition, and ignored treatment that could impede the progress of the disease. Imagine a person who supposed that he had a certain disease and took medicine for that condition when the reality was that he did not have the disease he thought at all and the medicine was doing significant harm to his system. Imagine a person who feels strongly that all religions are equal and that following any religion sincerely will bring a person to heaven. We are all familiar with the proverb, "The road to Hell is paved with good intentions," and we recognize that a correct understanding of reality is important in most areas of life.

This book has argued that every Christian's goal should be a worldview that is informed by both general and special revelation. We have maintained that Christians need to use the mental and perceptual faculties God has given them to the full as they seek to know and organize (that is, integrate) information derived from the various sources. We recognize that our understanding and interpretation is limited because we are finite and fallen beings. At the same time we would argue that it is possible to know many things, perhaps not with philosophical certainty, but with such a high degree of probability that one would be foolish to fail to respond. We have argued that Christians need to be aware of their worldviews that determine how they see things and how they organize and evaluate data that confronts them, and that conscious deliberate attention on our part is necessary to recognize many of those values and commitments. It is vital to be open to whatever discoveries are to be made as we live life and to be willing to adjust our thinking as that becomes necessary in the light of new information.

The goal of every Christian ought to be a worldview that is informed by Scripture. It is important to realize that while Scripture is true and authoritative, all our interpretations of it are not. We must recognize what is involved in the proper interpretation of God's Word, and we must diligently study and reflect on that truth so as to become skilled craftsmen at both interpreting and applying Scripture. There are many difficult passages in God's Word, and we will never understand Scripture in every detail. At the same time, as we have sought to demonstrate in this final chapter, there are many points made by Scripture that are stated with such clarity that believers diligently seeking to know God's truth can understand those teachings. Such truths should stand as core beliefs in the worldview of any biblically informed Christian. These declarations of Scripture stand in strong contrast to many of the assumptions and claims of both modernity[G] and postmodernism (and the zeitgeists of every other time, for that matter).

Christian thinking, difficult as it sometimes may be, is essential if we are to be the people God intends us to be, people who elevate God's reputation in all that we do. Such renewal comes as a part of sanctification which is a work of God but one which the Reformers remind us is "a work of God in which the believer cooperates." Diligence in using our minds is a part of the process and is essential if we are to love the Lord our God with all our mind as Jesus commanded (Matt. 22:37).

Questions For Further Consideration:

1. Make two lists. In the first, list those aspects of the zeitgeist that seem helpful in moving toward God's goal for you. In the second, list those aspects that are a hindrance. Look for a pattern in your lists. What have you learned?

2. The list below is taken from chapter 9's examination of the early chapters of Genesis. Taken together they comprise some beginning elements for a biblically informed worldview. Note one or more of these components that are not adequately represented in your worldview.

God's existence	God's sovereignty
God's separateness from his creation	People are created in God's image
God's power	God's wisdom
People are creatures	People's need for relationships
People's need for relationship with God	
	People are sinners
Redemption	

3. Assuming that at least one of the components above was inadequately represented in your worldview before reading this chapter, how might you integrate that neglected component into your worldview?

4. Are there worldview components from the list in question 2 that are not adequately represented in the current zeitgeist? What are the consequences of this neglect for our culture?

5. What specific steps do you intend to take to make progress in Christian thinking and in continuing to develop a biblically informed worldview? What are your goals for next month? For the next six months? For a year from now?

Notes

[1]Eugene Petersen, *A Long Obedience in the Same Direction* (Downers Grove, Illinois: InterVarsity Press, 1980), p. 11.

[2]Phillips and Brown, *Making Sense of Your World*, deal with the components of a biblically informed worldview in some detail. James Sire, *Discipleship of the Mind* (Downers Grove, Illinois: InterVarsity Press, 1990), presents what he considers to be the basic worldview questions and then compares and contrasts the way different worldviews answer the questions.

[3]J. I. Packer, "Hermeneutics and Biblical Authority," *Themelios* 1 (1975), p. 5.

[4]John Warwick Montgomery, "The Theologian's Craft," *Concordia Theological Monthly* 37 (1966), pp. 85-86, esp. nn. 71-72.

[5]Henri Blocher, *In the Beginning* (Downers Grove, Illinois: InterVarsity Press, 1984), p. 17.

[6]George W. Coats, *Genesis*, vol. 1, The Forms of Old Testament Literature (Grand Rapids, Michigan: Eerdmans, 1983), p. 47.

[7]James Montgomery Boice, *Genesis*, vol. 1 (Grand Rapids, Michigan: Zondervan, 1982), p. 33.

[8]The Hebrew word used here ('elillim) apparently is related to the Hebrew negative particle and is a derogatory term for idols; it means *nothing*. The irony comes from the fact that the word sounds very much like the word for god/God ('elohim).

[9]Wenham, *Genesis 1-15*, p. 27. Among the things that make this clear: the report of the creation of man comes at the end of the account and is the longest of the reports; the literary structure of the chapter seems to highlight man's creation as the climax; the evaluation (*very good*) that comes after the creation of man is different from that after the other reports (*good*).

[10]Alexander Altmann, "*Homo Imago Dei* in Jewish and Christian Theology," *Journal of Religion* 48 (1968), p. 235.

[11]Moshe Greenberg, "Some Postulates of Biblical Criminal Law," in *Studies in Bible and Jewish Religion Dedicated to Yehezkel Kaufmann on the Occasion of His Seventieth Birthday*, ed. by M. Haran (Jerusalem: Magnes Press, 1960), p. 15.

[12]See chapter 3, material referenced in note 19.

[13]Anthony Hoekema, *Created in God's Image* (Grand Rapids, Michigan: Eerdmans, 1986), pp. 5-6.

[14]Francis Schaeffer, *Genesis in Space and Time* (Downers Grove, Illinois: InterVarsity Press, 1972), p. 70

[15]*Ibid.* pp. 70-71.

[16]*Ibid.* p. 71.

[17]Hoekema, *Created in God's Image*, pp. 76-78.

[18]Kidner, *Genesis*, p. 63.

[19]There are many questions about how the kind of evil proposed by the serpent got into the world that God had declared *very good*. It is apparent elsewhere in Scripture that rebellion against God first took place in the angelic realm and that some of those inhabiting that realm seek to bring that rebellion and evil into the human realm.

[20]Von Rad, *Genesis*, p. 89.

[21]*Ibid.*, p. 97.
[22]See chapter 1.
[23]Montgomery, "Theologian's Craft," p. 90.
[24]Edward J. Palumbo, personal correspondence, July 1995.

GLOSSARY

Allegory/Allegorical Interpretation: Allegory is a type of literature in which incidents and characters in one realm actually represent those in a different realm. For example, Orwell's *Animal Farm* describes the activities and interactions between animals in a barnyard. What he is really describing, however, are events from a certain era in Russian history. Another example is Bunyan's *Pilgrim's Progress* where the Christian's pilgrimage from unbelief to maturity and finally to heaven is described in terms of a young man's journey. Allegorical interpretation involves reading a piece of literature as if it were allegory. Such interpretation either ignores the plain-sense meaning of the text in order to find meanings in another realm, or it seeks deeper spiritual meanings (that is, it spiritualizes the text) that go beyond what the text appears to say on the surface. For example, one might read an account of the Super Bowl (or a political campaign) as if it were a cosmic battle between the forces of light and darkness.

Autonomous Individualism: A characteristic of modernity in which the individual becomes the highest good and often the ultimate authority for what is true and good. Man does not bow to any higher authority, and man's opinion and judgment becomes the final arbiter of truth. This characteristic of modernity leads to the narcissism and selfishness that characterizes modernity. Such radical individualism leads to the elevation of the needs and desires of the individual above those of the community.

Coherence view of truth: This view argues that an understanding of reality is not really possible and argues that the best we can hope for is to have a system that does not have internal contradictions. Thus something is true if it fits together coherently with other views held to be true.

Control beliefs: These are the nonnegotiable beliefs and values. Under conditions of tension and conflict, these are the values that control a person's response. They are also sometimes called

Core Values because they are held at the very core of a person's being. It takes a great deal of evidence and cognitive dissonance to bring a person to the point of changing these beliefs. It is normally very traumatic to give up these basic beliefs and values. Regeneration brings about dramatic changes even in these values, and as 2 Corinthians 5:17 puts it, a person who is in Christ becomes "a new creature; the old things passed away; behold, new things have come."

Correspondence view of truth: The idea that truth is that which corresponds to reality. The view assumes that reality exists and that we can understand it at least to some degree.

Eisogesis: This is the opposite of Exegesis. It means to read into a text a meaning that is not really there. It involves bringing one's biases and assumptions to a text in such a way that the text is not allowed to communicate its message to the interpreter. Instead the interpreter reads the meaning that his assumptions cause him to expect from the text, and he finds there what he is looking for rather than what the text actually says.

Empirical: While this term can refer to knowledge gained through either scientific experiment or personal experience, it often refers to the Enlightenment approach to knowing that came to be a characteristic of modernity. In this sense it refers to knowledge that is derived through carefully devised and controlled experiments and stands in contrast to tradition based on more casual observation.

Epistemology: This is the study of how people know. It deals with the various ways by which people know, the strengths and weaknesses of each method, the certainty with which we know, the limits of knowledge, and similar topics.

Eschatology: This is the area of theology that deals with the study of last things such as the return of Christ, death, judgment, heaven, immortality, and so forth.

Exegesis: This is another word for interpretation. It means to read out of the text the meaning that is there. It stands in contrast with Eisogesis, in which an interpreter reads into the text his or her preconceived notions as to what the text should say.

Finitude: This term derives from *finite*, the opposite of *infinite*. It refers to man's limits as a creature. Man was created by God and he was created with certain limits. He cannot know as much as God; he cannot control all things. Even apart from the effects that sin and the Fall have had on man's ability to perceive and know truth, human beings are finite and limited in their abilities.

General revelation: While this term is often used in theology to refer to what can be known about God from the world he created, we are using the expression in a much broader sense here. The term here refers to what can be known about reality (God included) from studying the world and society.

Grammatical historical interpretation: This interpretive method is the one generally practiced by the Reformers and is the method most often used by Evangelicals today. The method applies the same interpretative principles to the biblical text as would be used in interpreting any modern written communication. The goal of the method is to understand what the original author intended to communicate to his audience in the text he wrote. This is done by giving careful attention to word meanings, grammar, and syntax, as well as to the historical and cultural background out of which the communication came. The method recognizes the use of metaphors, figures of speech, sarcasm, symbolic language, the emotional impact of words, type of communication, and so forth, and it attributes to these expressions the meaning they convey in ordinary communication.

Hubris: The arrogance and pride that comes from a refusal to acknowledge our finitude and dependence on God.

Integration: Integration involves putting together all the relevant bits of information available from both general and special revelation in order to contribute to a unified picture of reality.

Interpretive scheme: Our worldview creates a grid through which we filter all that we experience. Our worldview establishes an interpretive framework by which we process and organize data. This system influences (and can determine) what we accept as legitimate and what we reject as fallacious, how we organize and prioritize information, and so forth.

Metanarrative: This term refers to universal theories that tie widely disparate areas of knowledge together and give coherence to broad categories of data. It was the opinion of modernity that humans were fully capable of discovering these principles and that given enough time human reason would produce the kind of broad explanations that were based on such empirical evidence and irrefutable logic that everyone would have to acknowledge their truth. Postmodernism denies that such theories are possible and makes no attempt to find such explanations. Instead they are content with diversity, fragmentation and even contradiction as they study the world.

Metaphor/Metaphorical: A metaphor is a figure of speech in which one thing is compared to another. The Bible uses many metaphors to explain spiritual truth. For example, the church is compared to the temple; salvation is compared to a trial in a law court or with the adoption of a child by parents; human bondage to sin is compared to slavery and deliverance for sin to the redemption by which a slave received his freedom. Metaphorical interpretation is similar to allegorical interpretation in that literal descriptions are understood by interpreters as if they were metaphoric.

Modernity: Modernity refers to that complex of ideas that resulted from the Enlightenment. Characteristics of modernity include great confidence in the sort of knowledge that is based on empirical proof and irrefutable logic, the priority of individual judgment, and a distrust for tradition, including religious tradition and the Bible. While human achievement showed that premodern thinking about the possibilities of human understanding and accomplishment were wrong, modernity was also culpable in being overly optimistic about human potential. Modernity has contributed much to our understanding, but in denying the supernatural realm and in failing to properly appreciate human finitude and depravity, modernity has contributed many elements to the zeitgeist that Christians must reject.

Perspectivism: This idea, common in postmodern thought, believes that there is no such thing as absolute truth; rather, truth is just a matter of perspective. What each individual sees is the result of his or her background, social and political context, and so forth. No ultimate judgment can be made about the legitimacy of anyone else's perspective. Such views contribute to the radical relativism that often characterizes postmodernism.

Pluralism: The term literally means more than one. It refers to the wide range of options that confront people in our world. There are varying opinions about every subject and numerous choices in virtually every area. This plurality of options contributes to the frustration of living and thinking in the world. Some postmodernists argue that virtually all the options are legitimate, a position that contributes to the relativism that is characteristic of postmodernism.

Postmodernism: We are using the term postmodernism to include both the complex of ideas and circumstances that follow modernity and the various responses to modernity. The failures of modernity to deliver the certain and all-encompassing knowledge that it promised, or to engineer an ideal world based on its methods has given way to a skepticism that such knowledge and solutions can ever be achieved. Postmodernism emphasizes the impossibility of ever knowing truth about anything and expresses doubts that language would be capable of accurately expressing truth anyway. Postmodernism is characterized by disunity and diversity and often by a radical relativism that sees truth and morality as only the construction of a particular group of people at a particular time and in a particular place.

Premodern paradigms: The worldview that dominated in the time before the Enlightenment was characterized by a practical logic that was largely content with enough information to allow people to live effectively and accomplish what needed to be done. Tradition, including religious tradition and Scripture, played an important and often authoritative role in the thinking of the people. Observations were made sometimes with less than scientific precision, but such approaches were usually adequate for life. People believed in the spiritual realm and often brought

God into the picture to explain those things for which their casual observations or limited ability to observe could not account.

Reductionism: The practice of reducing complex phenomena to one or a few elements and then assuming that such simplification accounted for the phenomena in a comprehensive way. For example, a person's value is sometimes reduced to the amount of money possessed or power exerted or attractiveness or intelligence. A church's success is reduced to how many people attend each Sunday or to the size of their offerings or the size or value of their facility.

Relativism: This is the idea that there are no absolutes and virtually every idea or opinion is equally legitimate. In modernity morality in effect was relative because the methods of modernity (empirical methods and reason) provided no way to generate a consensus as to what was right or wrong. Postmodernism sees morality as relative since truth is unattainable and morality then becomes whatever a particular group decides it is.

Special revelation: In addition to the general way God has revealed himself to mankind through the world he has created, God also reveals himself in a special way as he interrupts the natural processes of nature and human knowing. God has revealed himself through miracles, through theophanies (special appearances to people in a variety of ways), through prophets he called and gave special messages to. The ultimate special revelation of God is found in Jesus Christ. The accurate and authoritative record of God's special revelation to his people is found in Scripture, which is an inspired record of various instances of God's revealing himself in these special ways.

Worldview: Our worldview is the complex of knowledge, opinions, assumptions, and so forth that determine the way we view the world around us. Wolfe has suggested that worldview works like a spider web. At the center of the web are beliefs and values to which we are deeply committed. These are nonnegotiable, and changes to these values are difficult to come by. Other values toward the edge of the web are held with less intensity, and they are much easier to change when new data suggests that they need to be adjusted. Elements in our worldview come from the totality of our experiences, both conscious and unconscious, and they come from parents, our culture, our education, our peers, the media, and so forth. For the Christian, the values revealed by God in Scripture should play a decisive role in forming a world-view.

Zeitgeist: The term means the *spirit of the age*, and it refers to certain ideas and opinions that characterize a culture at a particular time in history. These ideas are so deeply entrenched in the culture that virtually everyone takes them as given, often without much critical reflection about the ideas and values. Such ideas and values play a major role in the worldviews of individuals in the culture and often determine how people understand reality and respond to circumstances and ideas.

FOR FURTHER STUDY

"The Chicago Statement on Biblical Hermeneutics." *Journal of the Evangelical Theological Society* 25 (1982), 397-401.

"The Chicago Statement on Biblical Inerrancy." *Journal of the Evangelical Theological Society* 21 (1978), 289-96.

Allen, Diogenes. "The End of the Modern World," *Christian Scholar's Review* 22 (1993), 339-47.

Baird, Forrest, and Dale Soden, "Cartesian Values and the Critical Thinking Movement: Challenges for the Christian Scholar and Teacher," *Faculty Dialogue* 19 (1993), 77-90.

Barclay, Oliver R. *The Intellect and Beyond.* Grand Rapids, Michigan: Zondervan, 1985.

Blamires, Harry. *The Christian Mind: How Should a Christian Think?* London: SPCK, 1963.

Curtis, Edward. "Old Testament Wisdom: A Model for Faith-Learning Integration," *Christian Scholar's Review* 15 (1986), 213-27.

Curtis, Edward. "Some Biblical Contributions to a Philosophy of Education," *Faculty Dialogue* 21 (1994), 91-110.

Diehl, David. "Evangelicalism and General Revelation: An Unfinished Agenda," *Journal of the Evangelical Theological Society* 30 (1987), 441-55.

Fee, Gordon, and Douglas Stuart, *How to Read the Bible for All Its Worth.* Grand Rapids, Michigan: Zondervan, 1982.

Gaede, S. D. *Where Gods May Dwell.* Grand Rapids, Michigan: Zondervan, 1985.

Gill, David. *The Opening of the Christian Mind.* Downers Grove, Illinois: InterVarsity Press, 1989.

Gundry, Stanley. "Hermeneutics or Zeitgeist as the Determining Factor in the History of Eschatologies," *Journal of the Evangelical Theological Society*, 20 (1977), 45-55.

Henrichsen, Walter, and Gayle Jackson, *Studying, Interpreting and Applying the Bible*. Grand Rapids, Michigan: Zondervan, 1990.

Holmes, Arthur. *All Truth is God's Truth*. Grand Rapids, Michigan: William B. Eerdmans Publishing Company, 1977.

Holmes, Arthur. *Contours of a World View*. Grand Rapids, Michigan: William B. Eerdmans Publishing Company, 1983.

Holmes, Arthur, ed. *The Making of a Christian Mind*. Downers Grove, Illinois, 1985.

Jackson, Douglas. "The Rise of Evangelical Hermeneutical Pluralism," *Christian Scholar's Review* 16 (1987), 325-35.

Kuhatschek, Jack. *Taking the Guesswork Out of Applying the Bible*. InterVarsity Press, 1990.

Kuhn, Thomas. *The Structure of Scientific Revolutions*, 2nd ed. Chicago, Illinois: University of Chicago Press, 1970.

Lundin, Roger. *The Culture of Interpretation*. Grand Rapids, Michigan: Eerdmans, 1993.

McGrath, Alister. "Why Evangelicalism is the Future of Protestantism," *Christianity Today* (June 19, 1995), 18-23.

McMinn, Mark, and James Foster. *Christians in the Crossfire*. Newberg, Oregon: The Barclay Press, 1990.

Mercadante, Linda. "The Male-Female Debate: Can We Read the Bible Objectively?" *Crux* 15 (1979), 20-25.

Nash, Ronald H. *Worldviews in Conflict*. Grand Rapids, Michigan: Zondervan, 1992

Oden, Thomas. "On Not Whoring After the Spirit of the Age," in *No Gods But God*, ed. by Os Guinness and John Seel. Chicago, Illinois: Moody Press, 1992.

Olthuis, James. "On Worldviews," *Christian Scholar's Review* 14 (1985), 153-64.

Osborne, Grant. *The Hermeneutical Spiral*. Grand Rapids, Michigan: Baker Book House, 1992.

Packer, J. I. "Hermeneutics and Biblical Authority," *Themelios* 1 (1975), 3-12.

Phillips, Timothy R., and Dennis Okholm. *Christian Apologetics in the Postmodern World*. Downers Grove, Illinois: InterVarsity Press, 1995.

Phillips, W. Gary, and William E. Brown, *Making Sense of Your World*. Chicago, Illinois: Moody Press, 1991.

Pinnock, Clark. *Biblical Revelation*. Chicago, Illinois: Moody Press, 1971.

Poythress, Vern. *Science and Hermeneutics*. Grand Rapids, Michigan: Zondervan, 1988.

Ramm, Bernard. *Protestant Biblical Interpretation*. Grand Rapids, Michigan: Baker Book House, 1970.

Ryken, Leland. "The Creative Arts," in *The Making of the Christian Mind*, ed. Arthur Holmes. Downers Grove, Illinois, 1985.

Sandy, D. Brent, and Ronald L. Giese, Jr. *Cracking Old Testament Codes*. Nashville, Tennessee: Broadman & Holman, 1995.

Sire, James. *Discipleship of the Mind*. Downers Grove, Illinois: InterVarsity Press, 1990.

Sire, James. *The Universe Next Door*. Downers Grove, Illinois: InterVarsity Press, 1976.

Sproul, R. C. *Knowing Scripture*. Downers Grove, Illinois: Inter-Varsity Press, 1977.

Tate, W. Randolph. *Biblical Interpretation*. Peabody, Massachuetts: Hendrickson Publishers, 1991.

Walker, Andrew. *Enemy Territory*. Grand Rapids, Michigan: Zondervan, 1987.

Walsh, Brian. "Worldviews, Modernity and the Task of Christian College Education," *Faculty Dialogue* 18 (1992), 13-35.

Walsh, Brian J., and J. Richard Middleton, *The Transforming Vision*. Downers Grove, Illinois: InterVarsity Press, 1984.

Walsh, Brian J., and J. Richard Middleton. *Truth is Stranger Than It Used to Be*. Downers Grove, Illinois: InterVarsity Press, 1995.

Wilhoit, Mel R. "Faith and Learning Reconsidered: The Unity of Truth," *Faculty Dialogue* 9 (Fall 1987), 77-87.

Wolfe, David. *Epistemology: The Justification of Belief*. Downers Grove, Illinois: InterVarsity Press, 1982.

INDEX

A

B

C

D

E

N

O

P

R

BIBLICAL INDEX